OXFORD PREPARATION & PRACTICE *for*

Cambridge English Preliminary

EXAM TRAINER

with 7 practice tests

Contents

	Introduction	3
Preparation & Practice Test 1	Reading	8
	Writing	29
	Listening	37
	Speaking	51
Practice Test 2	Reading	62
	Writing	71
	Listening	73
	Speaking	79
Practice Test 3	Reading	82
	Writing	91
	Listening	93
	Speaking	99
Practice Test 4	Reading	102
	Writing	111
	Listening	113
	Speaking	119
Practice Test 5	Reading	122
	Writing	131
	Listening	133
	Speaking	139
Practice Test 6	Reading	142
	Writing	151
	Listening	153
	Speaking	159
	Audioscripts	162
	Answer key for Preparation	182
	Answer key for Practice Tests 1–6	186
	Sample answer sheets	205
	Photographs for Speaking Part 2 tasks	210

Introduction

This set of six printed practice tests and training activities comes with an additional online practice test (see card with access code). This material provides thorough preparation and practice for the *Cambridge English B1 Preliminary* exam. It is available with and without an answer key. The answer key provides a full explanation of correct and incorrect answers.

The first test in the book contains preparation pages with training for exam tasks in each paper. These preparation pages consist of several exercises which give candidates training in how to approach each task type and what to look for in the exam. There are also tips on exam technique.

To download audio for the Listening tasks in this book, go to:
www.oup.com/elt/oxfordpreparation

For more information about the exam, including sample papers and videos of students doing the Speaking test, go to:
www.cambridgeenglish.org

Reading

This paper consists of six parts and takes 45 minutes. In Parts 1–4, candidates are tested on their knowledge of the structure of English with a focus on vocabulary and grammar, while Parts 5–7 include longer texts with related comprehension tasks focusing on reading skills. This paper includes 32 questions in total.

	Task type	Number of questions and marks	What you do	What it tests
Part 1	Multiple-choice short texts	5 questions; 1 mark each	Answer each question about a short text by choosing one option from a set of three.	Understanding five short messages of different types.
Part 2	Matching	5 questions; 1 mark each	Match five descriptions of people to eight short texts.	Reading for specific information and detailed comprehension.
Part 3	Multiple choice	5 questions; 1 mark each	Answer each question about a long text by choosing one option from a set of four.	Reading for gist, inference and global meaning, attitude, opinions and feelings.
Part 4	Multiple-choice gapped text	5 questions; 1 mark each	Choose sentences from a set of eight options to complete five gaps in a long text.	Understanding of how texts are structured, including cohesion and coherence.
Part 5	Multiple-choice cloze	6 questions; 1 mark each	Choose one word from a set of four options to complete the gaps in a short text.	Accuracy with vocabulary, as well as elements of grammatical knowledge, e.g. complementation.
Part 6	Open cloze	6 questions; 1 mark each	Think of a single word that best fits each of the six gaps in a short text.	Knowledge and use of grammatical structures, phrasal verbs and fixed phrases.

REMEMBER!

- Read and follow all instructions carefully.
- Read each text and task through quickly before answering.
- If there is a question you can't answer, don't waste time worrying about it. Go on to the next question.
- You will not have time to read all texts in detail, and it isn't necessary to do so. Skim and scan texts for answers where possible.

Writing

This paper takes 45 minutes and consists of two parts. In Part 1, you must answer the question, which is always an email. In Part 2, you must choose one of two questions. One option is an article and the other option is a story. Each task carries equal marks.

	Task type	Number of words	What you do	What it tests
Part 1	Write an email.	about 100 words	Read the short email and four prompts. Write an email in response, making sure you use appropriate language and include the points from the four prompts.	Ability to agree, disagree, give opinions, make suggestions and explain in a clearly structured piece of writing using an appropriate register. The range and accuracy of tenses, expressions and vocabulary, and whether you have included all the content points.
Part 2	Write an article or a letter.	about 100 words	Read the announcement from a magazine or website and the first sentence of a story. Choose the question that suits you best and write your answer.	Ability to produce a clearly structured piece of writing in an appropriate style for the intended reader. The range and accuracy of your grammar and vocabulary, and whether you have answered the question.

REMEMBER!

- Spend a few minutes making a simple plan for each piece of writing. Decide on an appropriate style, layout and organization. Think about the content of paragraphs and the language you will use, e.g. verb tenses. Keep your plan in mind while writing.
- Don't spend more than half the time on your first answer.
- Make sure you answer all the points in the question appropriately.
- Check your writing by reading it through. Try to hear your own voice and 'listen' for mistakes. Check grammar, spelling and punctuation.

Listening

This paper consists of four parts and takes about 30 minutes. The recorded texts may include the following:

- Single speakers: radio announcements, parts of talks, informational talks or radio programmes, recorded messages.
- Two or more speakers: conversations at home or between friends, interviews with questions from a radio presenter.

The speakers will have a variety of accents. Background sounds may be included before the speaking begins to provide contextual information. Candidates are given time to read through the questions after they listen to the instruction. They also have six minutes at the end to transfer their answers to the answer sheet. They hear each recording twice. There are 25 questions in this paper.

	Task type	Number of questions and marks	What you do	What it tests
Part 1	Multiple-choice short texts	7 questions; 7 marks	Listen to seven short monologues or dialogues. For each one, answer a question by choosing one visual image from a set of three.	Ability to identify specific information.
Part 2	Multiple-choice short texts	6 questions; 6 marks	Listen to six short dialogues. Each has a context sentence, as well as a question or a sentence to complete and three options. For each one, choose the option which best answers the question or completes the sentence.	Ability to identify gist.
Part 3	Cloze	6 questions; 6 marks	Listen to a longer monologue and complete six gaps in a summary of the text with the missing word or words.	Ability to identify and record specific information.
Part 4	Multiple-choice long text	6 questions; 6 marks	Listen to an interview (two speakers) and answer each of the questions by choosing one option from a set of three.	Ability to identify gist, detail, attitudes and opinions.

REMEMBER!

- Listen carefully to the instructions on the recording.
- Try to predict as much as you can about the recording from the questions on the paper before you listen.
- Don't panic if you don't understand much the first time.
- Answer all the questions, even if you are not sure of your answer.

Speaking

This paper consists of four parts and takes approximately 12 minutes. There are normally two candidates and two examiners. One examiner just listens and assesses, while the other, the interlocutor, assesses, gives instructions and talks to the candidates.

You will be assessed on:

- accurate use of grammar, and range and use of vocabulary
- pronunciation
- interactive communication
- discourse management.

	Task type	Timing	What you do	What it tests
Part 1	Introductory phase	2 minutes	Answer the examiner's questions, giving factual or personal information.	Ability to interact in general and social situations.
Part 2	Individual 'long turn'	3 minutes	Speak individually for about 1 minute about a photograph you are given.	Ability to speak at length, describe people and activities using a wide range of vocabulary and organize language using simple connecting words.
Part 3	Collaborative task	4 minutes	You are given an imaginary situation and a set of visual prompts to discuss with your partner according to the examiner's instructions.	Ability to interact with another speaker, make and respond to suggestions, discuss alternatives, make recommendations and work towards agreement with your partner.
Part 4	Discussion	3 minutes	Answer questions related to the topic of the Part 3 task that the examiner asks.	Ability to talk about likes/dislikes, habits and preferences, give opinions and justify them and agree or disagree with your partner.

REMEMBER!

- The examiner will begin by asking you a few general questions about yourself. This is to help you relax.
- In Part 2, when you are given the picture, describe it in as much detail as possible. Imagine you are describing it to someone who can't see it. Don't speculate about the context or talk about any wider issues raised by the picture.
- Don't dominate the conversation. Allow your partner the opportunity to talk.
- In all parts, take the opportunity to show the examiner how good your English is. Do this by using a wide range of vocabulary and grammar, and by speaking fluently and with good pronunciation.
- Keep talking until the examiner asks you to stop, and stay calm.

Preparation

Preparation • Reading

At the beginning of the Reading paper, you will see some instructions and information, including the items in the box below. Knowing how each paper is set up will help you to feel more prepared on exam day.
Note: While some papers in the Preliminary exam allow time at the end to transfer your answers to the answer sheet, you won't have any extra time at the end of the Reading paper, so you need to answer all questions directly on the answer sheet.

INFORMATION FOR CANDIDATES
Read the instructions for each part of the paper carefully.
Answer all the questions. Each question carries one mark.
Write your answers on the answer sheet. Use a pencil.
You must complete the answer sheet within the 45-minute time limit for this paper.

Part 1

Part 1 of the Reading paper tests your ability to identify the main message of five very short texts on different topics. For each text, you have to choose the best summary statement from three options (**A**, **B** or **C**). The correct answer is paraphrased, that is, it uses different words to express the same meaning as the original text.

1 Begin Part 1 by looking carefully at each text. Thinking about where you would typically see these types of messages can provide clues that will help you to find the correct answer. Match the texts (**1–5**) with where you might expect to see them (**A–E**).

1

RE: Tomorrow
Hi Ken,
My racket is being repaired at the moment. Could you lend me yours for the match tomorrow?
Thanks, Leo

2

Take with meals twice daily for a fortnight. In the event of no improvement, contact your doctor.

3

Bargain!
Buy a pair of late-night tickets and get one free. Offer runs Mon–Fri only.

4

Danger! Keep away from cliff edge and remain on the hiking path at all times.

5

Downtown Dentist
+442899675347
Evan, don't forget about your appointment at 2.30 on Tuesday! Failure to cancel may result in full charges.

A in a national park ___
B in text messages on a mobile phone ___
C on a label on medicine ___
D in an email inbox ___
E in a cinema ___

2 Look at the texts in exercise 1 again. What is the purpose of each one? Identifying the reason for a text will help you to understand its message. Write the correct text numbers (**1–5**).

A Text number ___ is a reminder.

B Text number ___ gives instructions.

C Text number ___ is a request.

D Text number ___ is an advertisement.

E Text number ___ is a warning.

TIP
It's a good idea to try to understand what the text means *before* you read the three answer options.

Preparation

TIP: Synonyms
Remember: The answer options will not use the same words as the main text. Instead, you will find different words that have the same meaning. These are called synonyms.
Sometimes there are several synonyms for one word. For example, *afraid*, *frightened* and *scared* are all synonyms of each other – they all mean the same thing.

3 Vocabulary practice is good preparation for Part 1, especially working with synonyms. Use the words in the list below to complete the sentences about synonyms.

allowed as well attempt beside certain daily discuss fix in addition not permitted sure unbelievable underneath

1 **Incredible** and ___________ mean the same thing.
2 **Also** means the same as ___________ and ___________.
3 To **repair** means the same as to ___________.
4 The word ___________ means **every day**.
5 Something **definite** means something ___________ or ___________.
6 **Below** means the same as ___________.
7 To **try** and to ___________ have the same meaning.
8 To **talk about** something means to ___________ it.
9 **Next to** means the same as ___________.
10 **Forbidden** means that something is ___________ or not ___________.

4 Read the sentences. Choose the summary that is closest in meaning.

1 The concert is postponed until next Tuesday night.
   A The concert on Tuesday night has now been cancelled.
   B The concert will continue to run until next Tuesday night.
   C The concert will take place on Tuesday night instead.
2 Anyone who would like an evening meal must ask for it before the event.
   A You need to request dinner in advance.
   B Meals will be provided when the event ends.
   C Dinner is not available because of the event.
3 He's mainly vegetarian, but he's fond of salmon and tuna.
   A He doesn't care for main vegetables or any sea food.
   B He typically eats meat, vegetables, and two kinds of fish.
   C Mostly, he doesn't eat meat, but he likes some fish.

Preparation

Preparation • Reading

Part 2

This part of the paper tests your ability to identify and understand specific information. In the exam, you will see two sets of texts. The first set describes something that five different people want or need. In the second set, there is a text offering what each person wants plus three additional texts that do not match any of the people. Your task is to match each person with the text that is most suitable for his or her needs.

1 Make sure you understand how to do the task in Part 2. Complete these steps with the words and phrases from the list below.

cross them out   eight   five   mark them   three

- First, read the descriptions of the **1** ________ people. Read very carefully, and underline any key information about each person's situation and what they need.
- Next, read the **2** ________ texts. Underline any matches with the descriptions of the people. Try to identify the **3** ________ texts that will not suit anyone, and **4** ________ .
- Remember: The language that matches information between the descriptions and the texts may be paraphrased.
- Finally, check that you can successfully match each person with one of the texts. When you are satisfied with your answers, **5** ________ clearly on your answer sheet.

TIP
Make sure you take the whole text into consideration. Check that you are matching all of the needs specified in the description of each person. There may be texts that include some, but not all, of the points mentioned.

2 Vocabulary practice, such as recognizing parts of speech, will help to improve your reading comprehension. Sort these words into the correct columns in the table.

ability   affect   already   collect   emergency   guilty   interested   lately   marvellous   particularly   provide   salary

Nouns	Verbs	Adverbs	Adjectives

TIP
In Part 2, you need to practise the skill of scanning. Scanning is when you quickly read a text in order to find specific information.

3 Scan the sentences for the required items.

1 Scan and underline two adjectives.

Bernie wants to find a small hotel that is not too expensive.

2 Scan and underline two ages.

There is room for 25 students in the class. The course starts on 2nd May and is suitable for 15- and 16-year-olds.

3 Scan and underline two locations.

Pedro wants to have the party by the swimming pool, but several family members prefer the beach.

4 Scan and underline two verbs.

Marcus is studying at home because he's had a broken leg since last month's football match.

5 Scan and underline two times of day.

Kei and Joe are meeting on Thursday. Joe wants to meet at noon, but Kei isn't free until half past twelve. They might meet on Friday instead.

TIP: Linking words
Look out for linking words when you read the texts. Linking words, such as *however* and *although*, can signal an important difference between two points.

4 Read the description of each person and the texts. Then answer the questions.

1 ***Person:*** *Jaime wants to get a train to a nearby town at around six o'clock on Saturday evening. He needs to arrive before 7 p.m. to meet his friend for dinner.*
Text: *There is a train at 6.05 p.m., which goes to that town, and during the week it takes 45 minutes to get there. However, at the weekends it takes an hour and 20 minutes because it makes more stops.*

1 Can Jaime get a train to that town? yes / no
2 Is there a train on Saturday? yes / no
3 Does the train on Saturday leave around 6 p.m.? yes / no
4 Will it arrive by seven o'clock on Saturday evening? yes / no
5 Is this text a match for Jaime's needs? yes / no

2 ***Person:*** *Rebecca needs to get a flight to Paris early on Monday morning. She can't afford to pay more than £120.*
Text: *There are three flights to Paris every Monday. Although they all have available seats, the 6 a.m. flight only has one left, and it costs £200.*

1 Are there flights to Paris on Mondays? yes / no
2 Is there a flight early on Monday morning? yes / no
3 Is there a seat available on that flight? yes / no
4 Can Rebecca afford to buy a ticket for this flight? yes / no
5 Is this text a match for Rebecca's needs? yes / no

TIP
Sometimes a text seems like a perfect match at first, but when you read more closely, it may not be a good fit. When you are trying to match a text to a description, ask yourself questions like these to help you decide whether the text is, in fact, a good match.

Practice Test 1 • Reading

Part 2

For each question, choose the correct answer.

The people below want to go out for a meal on Friday.
On the opposite page there are descriptions of eight places to eat.
Decide which place would be the most suitable for the people below.

6 

Sasha is organizing a night out for a group of 20 people from work. They want food, music and dancing. Her company is paying, so they can't spend too much!

7 

Carlos is going out with his girlfriend. He's looking for a quiet restaurant which serves international food but doesn't cost too much. He likes places that don't have a live band playing or that the music volume allows you to keep conversation going.

8 

Henry and Clara are taking their daughter out to celebrate her 21st birthday. They want to go somewhere expensive and special which isn't too noisy. They'd like to stay somewhere overnight. Their daughter doesn't eat meat.

9 

Tanya and Sam have got two young children. They want to go to a restaurant in the early evening where they can feel comfortable with their children. They don't want to go anywhere too expensive. One of their children is allergic to nuts.

10 

Ayesha and Jane are both 17. They'd like to go somewhere lively where they can eat cheaply and listen to modern music. They're going to a party afterwards, so they aren't interested in late entertainment.

EATING OUT THIS FRIDAY

A The Carriage Hotel

Fine food in beautiful surroundings, the dining room at The Carriage Hotel is perfect for a special night out. Prices are high, although there is a small discount for guests of the hotel. The chef's speciality is healthy food and they offer a good selection of tasty vegetarian options.

B **Oliver's**

Oliver's is an expensive bar that serves evening snacks. The bar has recently been redecorated and has a very modern look. Friday night is jazz night, when some of the best names in jazz play live at the bar. There are plenty of clubs and hotels nearby if you're looking for a late night.

C **Queen's Head**

You can eat good, home-cooked food in a friendly environment every lunchtime in the Queen's Head pub. Prices are low and the pub has an excellent play area for children. The restaurant is closed in the evenings, but there is evening entertainment, including live bands. The pub also provides bed and breakfast.

D **Let's Go**

Let's Go is a modern café in the centre of town, which is particularly popular with young people. The burgers and pizzas are very good and the food isn't expensive. Pop music is played every night, so the café can get quite noisy. It closes every evening at ten.

E **Checkmate!**

Buy tickets for a new and exciting restaurant in the centre of town. Pay one price for a three-course meal, followed by a disco with all the latest sounds. Group bookings welcome. Special offer this Friday only: pay for eight tickets and get two free.

F Friday Feasts

Relax in a family restaurant with good food at cheap prices. Children eat free between six and seven, ordering from special menus including healthy fruit desserts. Play area and children's entertainer at weekends.

G **Lilian's Restaurant**

Lilian is the owner of this quality vegetarian restaurant, which serves a variety of international food. The restaurant isn't cheap, but the quality of the food is excellent. You can choose from a variety of delicious vegetarian dishes from around the world. Don't miss the bean burger or the mushroom sandwich. Listen to live bands playing music from around the world every Friday and Saturday night.

H *Chez Jean-Paul*

Voted best restaurant of the year for its delicious French food, good service, low prices and pleasant surroundings, Chez Jean-Paul is perfect for a quiet night out for couples. If you fancy a romantic dinner with a carefully selected playlist, this is the right spot for you and your partner.

Preparation

Preparation • Reading

Part 3

Part 3 tests your ability to read and answer detailed comprehension questions.
In Part 3, you read a longer text, which is always about an individual. It's usually written in the first person, which means the writer is talking about himself or herself and uses the pronoun *I*. But sometimes it's written in the third person, which means someone else is describing the individual, and uses the pronoun *he* or *she*. The text always expresses attitudes or opinions.
In this part of the paper, you need to use the reading skills of skimming – reading quickly for the overall gist, and scanning – reading quickly to find specific information.

You are required to answer five comprehension questions about the text, and you choose your answers from four options (**A**, **B**, **C** or **D**).

TIP: Inference
You might need to use inference to answer a Part 3 question. This means that the information is not directly stated in the text, but that there are clues that will lead you to the correct answer. For example:
- **Text:** I opened the front door and left my wet umbrella in the hallway.
- **Question:** What was the weather like that day?
- **Answer:** We can infer that it was raining because the writer had a wet umbrella.

1 Understanding what type of information you are being asked for will help you to identify the correct answers. Read the questions and choose the type of information they are asking for.

1 How did Chris feel after the concert?
A purpose
B feelings
C gist

2 What is the writer's view on the rainforest?
A opinion
B gist
C purpose

3 Who does Keiko live with?
A attitude
B gist
C detail

4 What does Antonia say about the argument?
A feelings
B attitude
C gist

5 How might people describe the text?
A attitude
B feelings
C global meaning

TIP
The first four questions always follow the same order as the information appears in the text. The fifth and final question in Part 3 is always a broader question based on the entire text, i.e. global meaning.

Preparation

2 Circle the correct options about the reading skills of skimming and scanning.

A You scan a text when you need to find **1 general gist / specific information**, such as a number or a date, or some other detail that you want to locate within the text. This is something that you do quite **2 fast / slowly**. You **3 read / don't read** every word in the piece. Instead, your eyes move quickly over the whole text looking only for the specific item that you want to find. You **4 probably won't / will probably** get the overall gist of the text because you are only focusing on the particular detail that you need.

B You **1 scan / skim** a text when you want to get a sense of the overall meaning, in other words, the main gist of the piece. You **2 read / don't read** every word carefully; instead, you look quickly at the title and the text to get the general idea of what it's about. You mainly look at content words, such as nouns and adjectives. You **3 pay / don't pay** close attention to grammatical words. You probably won't pick up on **4 specific details / gist** because you only want a general impression.

3 Read each text and question. Then choose the correct answer.

I'd always imagined that losing my job would be the worst thing that could ever happen to me. In reality, it gave me an unexpected sense of freedom, which was surprising.

1 How did the writer feel about becoming unemployed?
- **A** She was surprised that she felt so bad about it.
- **B** She really didn't expect that it would happen to her.
- **C** She was surprised to suddenly feel very free.
- **D** She was glad that she hadn't lost her job in reality.

People should never be nasty to each other. When a person is cruel, most of the time it's because someone they care about did the same thing to them, and they are in pain.

2 The writer believes that people who are unkind to others
- **A** are generally suffering, too.
- **B** don't care about anyone else.
- **C** have never been hurt themselves.
- **D** do the same thing over and over.

When I was a kid, my best friend, Pia, moved away with her family. The neighbours arranged a party and provided everyone with food and drink. My gift for Pia was a heart-shaped necklace.

3 What did the writer do for Pia?
- **A** She organized a party for Pia and her family.
- **B** She gave Pia a present of some jewellery.
- **C** She bought food and drink for the celebration.
- **D** She made her a pizza in the shape of a heart.

Jack Ferguson was not like other teachers. He encouraged his students to be curious, to ask difficult questions, and he inspired them to do well. He never got angry in class.

4 What might a former student of Jack Ferguson's say about him?
- **A** Mr Ferguson wasn't liked by the students or the other teachers.
- **B** The questions that Mr Ferguson asked us were always hard.
- **C** He was a calm teacher. I remember that he was usually patient.
- **D** Mr Ferguson was different. He had a very positive influence on us.

4 Match the type of information required (**A–D**) with the questions from the previous task (**1–4**).

- **A** global meaning ___
- **B** writer's opinion ___
- **C** specific detail ___
- **D** writer's attitude ___

TIP
Remember: Pay very close attention to the question. Each of the answer options may include some information from the text, but only one option answers the question in full.

Preparation

Preparation • Writing

Part 2a

In Part 2 of the Writing paper, you have a choice between two questions. You can choose to write an article or a story; you don't have to write both. If you want to write the article, here are some preparation and practice tasks and tips. You will be given an announcement from a website or a magazine. The announcement will ask for articles on a particular topic. It will include some questions on this topic which you have to answer in your article. You need to write around 100 words. The examiners want to see that you are able to organize your article and use appropriate tenses, expressions and vocabulary.

TIP: Approach
When you see the topic of the article, don't be tempted to start writing immediately. Stop and spend some time reading the announcement carefully. Underline the key information it asks for. Next, plan your article. Think about the points you want to make and the kind of vocabulary you will need. Then start writing.

1 You will see an announcement similar to this one. Read it carefully. Then, using the words from the list below, complete the notes about how to write an article in Part 2.

> We need your articles!
>
> **TECHNOLOGY**
>
> Everyone has a mobile phone, but we use our phones in different ways.
>
> Do you think that you rely on your phone too much? What do you most use it for?
>
> Do you prefer to text people or ring them? Why?
>
> **Write an article answering these questions and we will put it in our magazine!**

end enough mention most opinion paragraph reason start

You need to **1** __________ by stating your personal **2** __________ about your own mobile phone use. Try to follow this with a **3** __________ or example. Now write your answer to the next question. It's fine to **4** __________ the various ways in which you use your phone. However, that is not **5** __________ . You need to clearly state what you **6** __________ use your phone for. Start a new **7** __________ to express your preference about calling or texting people. Try to **8** __________ with a strong sentence that sums up your article.

2 Practise different ways of introducing your opinions and preferences. Based on the questions in the announcement in exercise 1, write sentences of your own using these phrases.

1 I really believe that ...
2 From my point of view, ...
3 To be honest, I wouldn't say ...
4 Without a doubt, I ...
5 I prefer X to Y.
6 My own preference is for ...
7 Personally, I prefer ...
8 I like to X, but I prefer to Y.

TIP: Choosing the article

For the article in Part 2, you will need to practise key phrases for writing about your habits, preferences, opinions, recommendations, etc. You also need to make sure you have a good range of vocabulary to write about the required topic.
Look at the heading at the beginning of the announcement, which is usually in bold or capital letters. Decide whether you know enough vocabulary to write a 100-word article about this topic. If it's a topic that you don't care about, you may have difficulty producing an interesting article on it.

3 Here are two versions, A and B, of articles in response to the announcement on the previous page. Read each one. Then answer the questions by writing *A*, *B*, *both* or *neither*. Circle or underline items in the two texts as you think about your answers.

A Without a doubt, I rely on my mobile phone too much. I know this because it's the first thing I look at every morning and the last thing I look at every night. Yesterday, I accidentally left my phone at home and, without it, I felt anxious all day! I use my phone for different things, but I check social media more than anything else.

Personally, I prefer texting people to phoning them. The reason is that people often find it more convenient to reply quickly to a text than to make a call.

One thing is certain ... I love my phone!

B I don't rely on my mobile phone too much. The mobile phone has been a great invention in the modern world. Mobile phones have changed our lives. Mobile phones are useful fun. My mobile phone makes me happy. It's better to phone people than to text them. I like talking on the phone. It's a good way to communicate and it's nice to hear the other person's voice. Phones make us feel more connected to each other.

1 ________ Which article has quite a lot of repetition?
2 ________ Which article answers all of the questions in the announcement?
3 ________ Which article doesn't use different paragraphs?
4 ________ Which article shares personal opinions about mobile phones?
5 ________ Which article has spelling and grammar mistakes?
6 ________ Which article might be too short?
7 ________ Which article uses key phrases to introduce opinions and preferences?
8 ________ Which article supports answers with clear examples or reasons?
9 ________ Which article goes off topic?
10 ________ Which article is a stronger answer to the Part 2 task?

TIP: Going off the point

Going off the point (or off topic) means including information that has no direct connection to the task or to the questions you were asked.
In Article A, the writer includes some extra information about forgetting his or her phone. That is useful because it makes the original answer stronger. In Article B, the writer describes how he or she feels about mobile phones. This is going off the point because the announcement doesn't ask us how we feel about phones.

4 Circle four phrases in Article A in exercise 3 which the writer uses to introduce one or more of the following:

- opinion
- reason
- preference

TIP

Try to keep your article interesting for the reader by not repeating the same language.

Preparation

Preparation • Writing

Part 2b

Question 3 tests your ability to write a story based on a supplied opening sentence. If you decide not to write an article in Part 2, you can write a story of around 100 words instead. You will be given a sentence, which you have to use to start your story. The examiners want to see that you are able to organize a story using appropriate tenses, expressions and vocabulary.

Choose this question in Part 2 if you enjoy imagining and telling stories. You won't know in advance what the supplied first sentence will be, but you can prepare for story writing in other ways. You can practise how to:
- plan and structure a story
- write in various past tenses
- include time expressions and linking words
- use a range of adjectives and adverbs.

TIP
There are different ways to structure or organize your story. You might begin with the main action, next give more detail and finally write a conclusion. Or you could begin with some background, then describe the action and then finish the story. Make sure the points you make are connected so that your story makes sense and is easy for the reader to follow.

1 Think about how you should approach the story. Then put these steps in order (**1–6**).

A ___ Finish the story in the third paragraph.
B ___ Plan your story.
C ___ Check your spellings, grammar and punctuation.
D ___ In the first paragraph, describe the background/situation.
E ___ Read the opening sentence.
F ___ Develop the story with more details in the second paragraph.

2 Stories are usually written in the past tense. Make sure you know how to form different past tenses and when to use them. Match the descriptions (**1–3**) with the tenses (**A–C**).

1 This tense is used to show when an action or event in the past happened before another action or event in the past.
2 This tense is used to describe an action that started and finished at any time in the past, recent or distant.
3 This tense is used to describe an action or event which started in the past and went on for some time. It is often used for background information.

A ___ past simple
B ___ past continuous
C ___ past perfect

TIP: Time expressions
Make your story more interesting by introducing unexpected events. There are expressions you can use to signal these events. And your story will be easier to follow if you make it clear when various events are happening. Practise using expressions like *All at once*, *Just then*, *At that very moment*, *All of a sudden*, etc.

TIP: Focusing on the first line
Check the language in the supplied first line. If it's written in the past tense, don't switch to the present or future. Make sure you are using the correct pronoun.

3 Read this story. Circle the verbs in the past continuous. Underline the verbs in the past perfect. Draw a square around the verbs in the past simple.

I was in my bedroom when the storm began. It had been a very hot day and all the windows in the apartment were open. Everyone else had gone to the beach, but I didn't join them because I was studying for an exam.

Suddenly the wind and rain were crashing through our windows! It was loud and terrifying. I rushed from room to room. I closed every window. Then, as soon as I had finished, the storm ended unexpectedly.

Everything was calm again … until I heard another noise. A strange sound was coming from the kitchen. I screamed.

TIP: Improving your story
Remember that stories need to be enjoyable to read. One way to make your text better is to include a variety of adjectives and adverbs. Adjectives give us more detail about people and things. Adverbs give us more details about the action happening in the story.

4 Read the Part 2 story in italics. Then complete the new version of the story below with the adjectives and adverbs from the box. Do you notice any other improvements?

No one told me it had been cancelled. Ben Smith had organized a party for our friends, and I wanted to see everyone again.

That night, I spent ages getting ready because I wanted to look nice. I'd been looking forward to this. I bought new clothes for the occasion.

When I arrived at Ben's house, I walked up the steps and knocked on the door. But everything was quiet. The place was dark. I realized there was no party. I walked away. I felt sad.

brand   completely   excitedly   incredibly   miserable   slowly   specially

No one told me it had been cancelled. Ben Smith had organized a party for our old friends, and I was **1** ________ excited about seeing everyone again.

That night, I spent a long time getting ready because I wanted to look my best. I'd been looking forward to this for months! I bought **2** ________ new clothes **3** ________ for the occasion.

When I arrived at Ben's house, I rushed up the steps and knocked on the door **4** ________ . But everything was silent. The place was **5** ________ dark so I realized there was no party. I walked away **6** ________ . I felt **7** ________ .

TIP
Practise writing 100 words quickly. See how many lines this takes up in your handwriting. Make sure you have enough time to read your story and check that it's well organized. Check your grammar, spellings and punctuation, too.

Practice Test 1 • Writing

Part 2

Choose **one** of these questions.
Write your answer in about **100 words**.

Question 2

You see this notice in an English-language magazine.

> We need your articles!
>
> BOOKS
>
> What kind of books do you like to read?
>
> Do you prefer reading paper books or e-books? Why?
>
> Write an article answering these questions and we will put it in our magazine!

Write your **article**.

Question 3

Your English teacher has asked you to write a story.
Your story must begin with this sentence:

There was no one at the party when I arrived.

Write your **story**.

Preparation • Listening

At the beginning of the Listening paper, you will see some instructions and information, including the items in the box below. It's a good idea to be familiar with this information before the exam. When you know what to expect, you will feel more prepared.

INFORMATION FOR CANDIDATES
Listen to the instructions carefully.
Answer all the questions. Each question carries one mark.
You will hear each piece twice.
You will have six minutes at the end of the test to copy your answers onto the separate answer sheet. Use a pencil.

Part 1

Part 1 of the Listening paper tests your ability to listen for specific information. You will hear seven short recordings. You have to answer a question about each one by choosing the correct picture from three options.
There will be a short pause before the recordings are played. Use that time to look at the questions and the pictures. The recordings are played twice. Try to answer each question the first time you listen. The second time, listen and check your answers.

TIP
When you read the questions, make sure you understand what you are being asked. Look carefully at all the pictures in advance and think about what each represents.

1 Match the pictures (**A–C**) with the written descriptions (**1–3**).

1

A B C

1 seventeenth ___
2 fourteenth ___
3 fifteenth ___

2

A B C

1 shopping in the town centre ___
2 dancing at a party ___
3 watching a film at the cinema ___

3

A B C

1 having a picnic in the park ___
2 reading a book in the garden ___
3 sunbathing on the beach ___

4

A B C

1 booking a holiday over the phone ___
2 booking a holiday at a travel agency ___
3 booking a holiday online ___

5

A B C

1 two o'clock ___
2 four o'clock ___
3 one o'clock ___

Preparation

Preparation • Listening

Part 4

Part 4 of the Listening paper combines all the listening skills you practised in the previous parts.
You will hear a longer text, which is always an interview. The interview will be played twice. You will be asked six questions with three answer options, respectively, to choose from. You need to listen for gist and the overall context, as well as listening for specific information and details.
At the beginning of Part 4, before the recording is played, there will be a pause of 45 seconds. Use this time to read the questions and the answer options. Think about what you are being asked in each question so that you can listen carefully for the information you need.

1 Here are some questions and answer options typical of what you might find in Part 4. Read them carefully. Then circle the correct type of information that each question is asking for.

1 What is Gerry's blog about?
- **A** extreme sports
- **B** winning and losing
- **C** fun and games

This question asks for **an opinion / overall gist**.

2 Gerry didn't enjoy rollerblading because
- **A** he was very tired that day.
- **B** he didn't feel safe enough.
- **C** he thought he looked silly.

This question asks for **detailed meaning / someone's attitude**.

3 What does Gerry say about readers of his blog?
- **A** They have been extremely supportive.
- **B** He communicates with them regularly.
- **C** Every reader is very important to him.

This question asks for **general gist / specific information**.

4 Next year, Gerry is planning to
- **A** set up a new website.
- **B** travel to South Africa.
- **C** do more interviews.

This question asks for **specific information / someone's opinion**.

5 Gerry didn't enter the competition because
- **A** he was too busy with other projects.
- **B** he wanted to build up more followers.
- **C** he hadn't heard about it in enough time.

This question asks for **someone's attitude / detailed meaning**.

6 What does Gerry think of video blogs?
- **A** He feels they're too noisy.
- **B** He's not sure about them.
- **C** He thinks they're exciting.

This question asks for **someone's opinion / general gist**.

TIPS
- Some of the items in Part 4 are in question form, and some are sentence completion.
- Look closely at the language in each one and ask yourself: *Do I need to listen for someone's attitude or opinion, or for a specific detail?*
- In the questions, look for words like *think, feel, because* and *say*.

TIP
Remember: The answer options will paraphrase what the speaker said. If you read or hear a word that you don't understand, don't panic. You can usually work out the meaning from context.

2 Match the questions (**1–6**) with the text that answers them (**A–F**).

1 How did she start working as a game designer? ___
2 She doesn't think gaming is a bad thing because .... . ___
3 How does she usually get her ideas? ___
4 She is grateful to .... . ___
5 What does she say about her free time? ___
6 Her hopes for the future are .... . ___

A That really happens as a team. I mean, we sit down together and discuss different possibilities. We all make suggestions. It kind of develops from there.

B Oh, I generally don't think that far ahead! I just take things one day at a time. Right now, I'm happy with the business, but, I don't know, maybe in a year or two I might like to start giving courses on gaming. We'll see.

C Well, I'm not really into sport in general, but I love yoga. I do it three evenings a week and I find it very relaxing. I'm busy most weekends, but when I can, I meet my friends for lunch or dinner.

D Originally, I wasn't going to be a game designer. I was actually doing a degree in maths! A friend of mine was developing a video game and he asked me to help because I knew how to write code. That's how it all began!

E I have so much to thank my mother for. She always encouraged me to believe in myself. And she inspired me to try new things. She's amazing!

F Some people are very negative about it. I know that. But there are a lot of positive aspects to this industry as well! I'm proud of creating something that others can enjoy. It makes people think quickly, and it's fun!

3 **07** **Studying the questions and knowing what information you need to listen for is very important. It is equally important to know what information you can ignore. Listen to the excerpt from this interview. Read each question and the summary of statements (A–G). Then cross out the ones that do not help you to answer the question.**

1 What does the woman say about fans and followers?
- **A** 10,000 people follow her online.
- **B** There's nothing special about 10,000.
- **C** She feels good about what she has achieved.
- **D** Others have hundreds of thousands!
- **E** She wants to do better.
- **F** Some people have millions.
- **G** Teenage girls typically follow her.

2 How does the woman feel about her success?
- **A** She has 10,000 online followers.
- **B** It's fairly common to have 10,000 followers.
- **C** She is proud of her achievement.
- **D** She's happy, but she wants to do more.
- **E** There are people with millions of followers.
- **F** A lot of teenage girls follow her.
- **G** Some boys have started to follow her, too.

Practice Test 1 • Listening

Part 4

08 For each question, choose the correct answer.

You will hear a woman called Alice Parker talking on the radio about a new shop.

20 What kind of business has Alice started?
- **A** a restaurant
- **B** a shop with a café
- **C** a travel agency

21 Why did she decide to start the business?
- **A** She wanted to make a lot of money.
- **B** She wanted some experience of selling.
- **C** She wanted to be independent.

22 When did she decide to start a business?
- **A** when she was abroad
- **B** when she was shopping in England
- **C** when she lived in India

23 When she goes abroad, she chooses items that are
- **A** expensive.
- **B** unusual.
- **C** easy to carry.

24 What is Alice planning to do soon?
- **A** open another shop
- **B** employ more people
- **C** sell more food

25 What does Alice dislike about her new business?
- **A** the number of hours she works
- **B** difficult customers
- **C** having to travel

Preparation • Speaking

INFORMATION FOR CANDIDATES
The Preliminary Speaking paper is the only section of the exam where you do not write anything down. For this reason, it is important to listen carefully to the questions you are asked, and to speak clearly when you answer.
You will be in a room with one other candidate. There will be two examiners in the room.
One examiner is the interlocutor – this is the person who will ask you and your partner questions. He or she will have some packs of materials.
The other examiner is the assessor – this is the person who assesses your answers and assigns your marks. The assessor does not participate in any of the conversations.

Part 1

Part 1 is the shortest part of the Speaking paper. It lasts for about two minutes.
It tests your ability to communicate about everyday things. In this part of the test, you do not interact with your partner.
There are two phases, or sections, in this part. In Phase 1, the interlocutor will ask you some short questions about yourself. You will usually be asked for personal information such as your name and where you live.
In Phase 2, the questions require slightly longer answers. For example, you might be asked about something you like or dislike, and asked to explain why.

TIP
If you don't hear a question clearly, it's OK to ask the interlocutor to repeat it.

1 Use the words in the list below to complete the Phase 1 questions. Four words are not used.

Are Do in like name spell What Where Who with

1. What's your ________ ?
   Chris
2. ________ is your surname?
   Potter
3. How do you ________ it?
   P-O-T-T-E-R
4. ________ do you come from?
   Canada
5. Who do you live ________?
   my mother and brother
6. ________ you study?
   yes

TIP
Sometimes when we feel nervous, we say too much or too little! Even though you might feel nervous, try not to give one-word answers in this part of the test. You don't need to give very long answers, but make sure you form whole sentences.

Preparation

2 Use the information from exercise 1 to write full answers.

1 ______________________
2 ______________________
3 ______________________
4 ______________________
5 ______________________
6 ______________________

3 Make sure you use the correct tense when you answer the questions you are asked. Read these questions and choose the tense they should be answered in.

1 Where are you from?
   A past
   B present
   C future
2 What did you do last week?
   A past
   B present
   C future
3 Have you got a job?
   A past
   B present
   C future
4 What are your plans for this weekend?
   A past
   B present
   C future
5 How long do you spend working/studying every day?
   A past
   B present
   C future
6 Where did you go on holiday last year?
   A past
   B present
   C future

4 Work with a partner to ask and answer the questions in exercise 3.

5 09 Read these typical Phase 2 questions (**A–D**). Then listen and match each answer (**1–4**) with the correct question.

A What do you like doing with your friends? ___
B Tell us about a celebrity you like. ___
C How often do you use your mobile phone? ___
D Which do you like better, Saturday or Sunday? ___

TIP
Notice how the speakers responded. They answered the questions they were asked and, without speaking for too long, they also provided some supporting information, such as reasons or examples.

Preparation • Speaking

Part 2

Part 2 of the Speaking paper lasts for about two minutes.
You will be given a photograph and asked to talk about it for around one minute. You are required to describe what you see in your photo.
Your partner will be given a different photograph, which he or she will talk about for one minute, too. In this part of the test, you do not interact with your partner.

TIP
When you first see your photograph, try to begin with a general sentence about the overall scene. After that, you can go into more detail describing specific things and people in it.

1 A good approach to Part 2 is to imagine you are describing your photo to someone who can't see it. For this reason, it's important to explain where things are in the photo. Write *at*, *in* or *on* to complete these prepositions of place.

1 ___ the top of the photo
2 ___ the right
3 ___ front of the ...
4 ___ the top right corner
5 ___ the bottom of the photo
6 ___ the middle
7 ___ the left
8 ___ the background

2 Part 2 tests your ability to use a range of vocabulary. Try to include adjectives to make your description more interesting, but don't keep repeating the same ones. Choose **two** words (**A–C**) that mean the same as each adjective (**1–6**).

1 happy
A delighted
B confused
C cheerful

2 strange
A unexpected
B unusual
C unnecessary

3 huge
A very big
B intelligent
C enormous

4 sad
A charming
B unhappy
C miserable

5 pretty
A lovely
B nice
C keen

6 ordinary
A simple
B nervous
C plain

TIP
If you can't think of the right word for something in your photograph, don't give up. Try to use other words to describe it.

Preparation

3 Draw lines to match the adjectives (**1–6**) with their opposites (**A–F**).

1	modern	**A**	rude
2	confident	**B**	fun
3	terrible	**C**	nervous
4	noisy	**D**	wonderful
5	polite	**E**	old-fashioned
6	boring	**F**	quiet

4 The tenses you will mainly use in Part 2 are the present simple and the present continuous, so it's a good idea to practise using them. Read this description of a photograph. Write the correct form of the verbs in brackets.

This **1** __________ (be) a photograph of a camping trip. It **2** __________ (look) like fun! On the left of the photo, there's a large tent. On the right, there **3** __________ (be) four people. They **4** __________ (have) a picnic. Three of them are sitting on a blanket. The other person **5** __________ (stand) up. He **6** __________ (have) a mobile phone in his hand. In the background, I can see a river or a lake and several small boats on the water.

TIP

When you are describing your photograph, just talk about the things you can actually see in it. You don't need to make guesses about the situation or context.

5 Look at the pictures. Complete the descriptions with the words and phrases from the list below.

background concentrating hard foreground getting up helmet holding onto it in the air long-sleeved top number 23 jersey number 7 on the ground reaching down

This photograph shows a scene from a football match. It looks like an exciting game! In the **1** __________, I can see two players. The nearest one is wearing the **2** __________, which is dark blue. He's also wearing white shorts and long blue socks. He's on the ground, but it looks like he's **3** __________. The other person I can see is the **4** __________ player. He's wearing a white jersey with red shorts and long white socks. He's actually **5** __________, and so is the ball! I think he's about to kick it. I can see that he's really **6** __________. The football stadium is in the background. It's completely full of fans! I know it's night-time because the stadium lights are on.

In this picture, I can see that there's been a road accident. There's a woman lying on the road. She's wearing a **7** __________, and her right leg is injured or sore because she's **8** __________. Luckily, it doesn't seem to be too serious because she's sitting up. Her bicycle is lying **9** __________ behind her. In the bottom right corner of the photo there is a white bicycle **10** __________. In the middle of the picture there's a man wearing a blue jumper. He's **11** __________ to help the woman, and he's also talking on his mobile phone. Right behind him there's a dark-coloured car with one door open. In the **12** __________, there are some buildings.

Practice Test 1 • Speaking

Part 1

Phase 1: Select one or more questions from this list.

Personal details

- What's your name?
- What's your surname?
- How do you spell it?
- How old are you?
- Where do you live?
- Who do you live with?

Phase 2: Select one or more questions from each of the following categories.

Everyday life

- Have you got a job?
- What job do you do? / What subjects do you study?
- How do you get to school / work every day?
- Do you think that English will be useful for you in the future?

Free time

- What do you do in your free time?
- What did you do last weekend?
- What are your plans for this weekend?

Part 2

1 **On an outing**

2 **Travelling**

Candidate A Look at the photo on page 210. It shows people on an outing. Say what you can see in the photo.

Candidate B Look at the photo on page 211. It shows people travelling. Say what you can see in the photo.

Preparation

Preparation • Speaking

Part 3

Part 3 of the Speaking paper lasts for about four minutes.
In this part, you have a discussion with your partner. The interlocutor will describe an imaginary situation for you to discuss. To help the discussion along, you will be given some ideas in the form of pictures. With your partner, you discuss the situation and, ideally, come up with the best idea.
Your task is to make and respond to suggestions, to discuss other possibilities and to try to reach an agreement.

---

1 Think about how you should approach this exercise. Then put the following steps in order (**1–6**).

A ___ Make suggestions.
B ___ Listen to the interlocutor.
C ___ Respond to ideas.
D ___ Look at the pictures.
E ___ Reach an agreement.
F ___ Begin the discussion.

2 There are key phrases you will need to use when you make suggestions and agree or disagree with your partner. Complete the table with the expressions in the box.

How about ... ? I don't think that would work. I think you're right.
I'm afraid I don't agree. It's a great idea. Maybe we could ...
Sorry, I don't see it that way. That's true because ... Well, I disagree because ...
What if we ... Why don't we ... Yes, I agree with that.

Agreeing	Disagreeing	Making suggestions

3 Read these sentences. Cross out the ones that are inappropriate because they aren't polite.

1 Oh yes, that's an interesting suggestion.
2 That's wrong. We should do it this way instead.
3 No. I have a much better plan.
4 I understand. Unfortunately, I think it might be difficult to manage.
5 I can see the advantages, but there could be some issues.
6 It's obvious that would never work. Luckily, I have an excellent idea.

TIP
Whenever you make a suggestion, invite your partner to say what he or she thinks of it.

TIP
It's very important to remain polite during the discussion. Listen carefully to what your partner says, and be respectful when you disagree or make alternative suggestions.

4 The interlocutor has given two candidates an imaginary situation to discuss. The situation is that some local families in the town have lost their homes in a fire. You and your partner want to hold a charity event to help the families, but you don't have much time to organize it.
You are given this visual prompt and asked to discuss the ideas. Your task is to discuss the possibilities and, together, decide which would be the best to do and the quickest to arrange.
Look at the ideas. Think about the pros and cons (advantages and disadvantages) of each one.

> **TIP**
> Remember: In the exam, the ideas will be presented in pictures rather than words.

5 Read these excerpts from a discussion between two candidates. Circle the word or phrase that is better to use in this part of the exam.

1 **Me / Personally**, I like the idea of a sports day. Most people enjoy sports, and it would be fun. **And you? / What do you think?**
2 **Definitely / Maybe** we could arrange a charity car wash instead. **Am I right? / How does that sound to you?**
3 Yes. **I see what you mean. / I know.** You're right. How do you **think / feel** about the idea of a cake sale, then?
4 I'm just not sure we'd make much money selling cakes. **Do you agree? / Yes?**
5 Yes, I do. Good point. So, **what's going on? / what do you think we should do?**
6 As far as I'm **concern / concerned**, a quiz is the best option.

6 10 Now listen and check your answers. You will hear the complete discussion.

> **TIPS**
> - It's OK if you don't discuss every idea in the visual prompts, but try to consider as many as possible.
> - Do your best to reach an agreement before the time is up.
> - Remember: You can also suggest alternative ideas of your own.
> - When you make a point, try to provide a reason for it. Explain why you believe an idea will or won't work.

Preparation • Speaking

Part 4

The final part of the speaking paper lasts for about three minutes.
Part 4 always links to Part 3. You and your partner will now be asked follow-up questions on the same topic as you discussed in Part 3. You may be asked for your opinion on this topic or your own experiences, habits or preferences related to it. Sometimes you will be asked questions individually, but the interlocutor will also address questions to both of you. You are expected to communicate with each other when you are answering.

---

1 The questions in this part of the test are spoken, not written down, so you need to listen carefully and think about what you are being asked. Read these typical follow-up questions related to the topic in Part 3. Choose the objective of each question.

1 Do you think that events for charity are important? (Why?)
- **A** habits
- **B** likes/dislikes
- **C** personal opinion

2 Have you ever taken part in a charity event?
- **A** agree/disagree
- **B** personal experience
- **C** preference

3 Which do you think is better: making the government or the public responsible for charity?
- **A** preference
- **B** habit
- **C** experience

4 Do you enjoy supporting charity events? (Why?)
- **A** likes/dislikes
- **B** recommendation
- **C** agree/disagree

2 Underline the words or phrases in the exercise 1 questions that helped you answer.

3 Match the statements (**1–6**) with their functions (**A–F**).

1 From my point of view, this is a very positive development. ___
2 While online groups can be useful, I would rather meet other members in person. ___
3 I worked on a project like this about a year ago. It was incredibly interesting. ___
4 Yes. I, too, feel it's true that more people need to get involved. ___
5 I appreciate their efforts, but I really don't enjoy surprises. ___
6 Every day, I bring my own cup to the café, and I generally recycle as much as I can. ___

- **A** agree/disagree
- **B** habits
- **C** personal opinion
- **D** likes/dislikes
- **E** preference
- **F** personal experience

TIP

When one of the candidates has answered a question, the interlocutor may turn to the other candidate and ask: *How about you?* or *What do you think?* or *Do you agree?* Revise the agreeing/disagreeing phrases you practised in Part 3.

Preparation

4 Use the words and phrases in the box to complete these sample answers.

don't agree experience explain far go along mean point

1. From my ___________, people are usually willing to help.
2. I think it's a dangerous idea. Let me ___________ what I mean.
3. It's a popular issue. I ___________, most people have thought about it.
4. I know it's a worry, but there's still hope. I ___________ that it's too late to change it.
5. As ___________ as exercise is concerned, I definitely don't do enough.
6. I can't ___________ with that idea because it won't change anything.
7. The ___________ I'm making is that we all have responsibilities.

5 Giving clear answers is your first goal, but you should also use a range of language. Make these answers more interesting by inserting the adverbs in the correct place.

1. If you ask, everyone will help. (nicely)
2. It's difficult at the beginning. (always)
3. They shouldn't drive so fast. (really)
4. It seems to be an expensive operation. (extremely)
5. It's a product I would buy for my parents. (definitely)

6 Read the questions. Which answer do you think is better, A or B?

1. Do you think that events for charity are important? (Why?)
   - **A** *Yes because they help people. Sometimes they're fun. Well, you can't always have fun at charity events, but sometimes you can, and that's OK, I think.*
   - **B** *In my opinion they're very important. The reason is that there are people in the world who are suffering, and, without charity events, they would suffer even more.*
2. Have you ever taken part in a charity event?
   - **A** *Yes, I took part in one last year. A local charity needed a new van, and a group of us wanted to help. We played table tennis for 24 hours and people gave us money for it.*
   - **B** *Yes, I did an event for charity a few weeks ago. My cousin did it with me. He lives in Mexico but he was visiting me in London. I don't see him often so it was exciting!*
3. Which do you think is better: making the government or the public responsible for charity?
   - **A** *The way I see it, charity is entirely the responsibility of the government. And I don't like it when politicians don't do their job, but unfortunately it happens all the time.*
   - **B** *As far as I'm concerned, it should be both. It shouldn't stop with politicians because society is better when members of the public help each other.*

TIPS

- Don't worry if your opinions are right or wrong. Show that you can participate in a conversation and use a wide range of language to express yourself.
- Don't just answer *Yes* or *No*. Explain what you mean and give examples.
- Show interest in what your partner is saying.

Practice Test 1 • Speaking

Parts 3 and 4

Taking up a new sport

Part 3

A young man wants to do more exercise, but he doesn't have a lot of money. He wants to find a sport that he can do to get fit.

Look at the opposite page. Here are some sports that he could take up.

Talk together about the different sports, and say which would be the cheapest to do and the best for keeping fit.

Part 4

Answer and discuss together the following questions:

- What sports have you played?
- Which sports do you play now?
- Did / Do you enjoy these sports?
- Do you think it is important to play sports? Why (not)?

Practice Test 2 • Reading

Part 2

For each question, choose the correct answer.

The people below all want to go to a restaurant or café.
On the opposite page there are some restaurant reviews.
Decide which restaurant or café would be the most suitable for the people below.

6 José is on a special diet and needs to eat a lot of vegetables. He doesn't have a lot of money. He likes eating outside because he usually studies indoors.

7 Sarah leads a very busy life and so chooses places where the service is fast. She likes to eat healthy food and loves fresh fruit and vegetables. She often orders the vegetarian option in the menu.

8 Karl enjoys eating out in places with good music and an interesting mood. He loves untypical food and often enjoys going to a spectacular location by car to get something special.

9 Fernando wants to take his girlfriend out for a meal in a special restaurant and doesn't mind about the cost. He wants to walk home, so it must be close to the city centre. He'd like to surprise her with his choice of restaurant.

10 Linda and Barry want to take their children to a restaurant with live music for an evening out. They need a menu with a variety of options and are happy to pay a bit more for excellent food.

OUR TOP EIGHT RESTAURANTS

A Luigi's

This is a beautiful Italian restaurant with soft lighting and a lot of candles – an excellent place for a night out with that special person in your life. The food was delicious, but we found the music made it difficult to have a conversation.

B Bob's Barbecue

You have to try Bob's Barbecue on the beach. It's fantastic food – tasty fish dishes, sausages and steaks grilled on the fire. There's always good pop music playing, and often a live band performs. This wasn't cheap, but the kids' menus offer a wide choice and are really good value.

C *Green Dreams*

Everything served in this busy little restaurant is vegetarian. If you think food that's good for you might be boring, you'll be pleasantly surprised. Fresh vegetables are used in a variety of interesting ways. However, we had to wait quite a while for our food.

D The Great Castle Dining Hall

For a more unusual dining experience, drive out to this castle, which is high in the mountains, and eat like the rich families of 1,000 years ago. You'll be served a six course meal of delicacies from that time. The waiters all dress in authentic costumes and musicians add to the atmosphere.

E Grandma's Kitchen

You won't find any unusual food here, just good old-fashioned recipes like Grandma used to make, although prices seem to have gone up a bit since her day. Roast beef with potatoes was our favourite here. This is a good place to step back in time.

F Paradise Café

The Paradise Café offers a good varied menu to suit many tastes without you needing to spend too much. Try the carrot and spinach soup and the freshly picked salads. Sink into their comfortable sofas or enjoy the summer weather in the garden. It can get quite busy in the evening so book early to avoid disappointment.

G The Hollywood Restaurant

This was the first time we'd been to a restaurant with its own cinema! The Hollywood is located in the centre of the city and is a surprisingly private little place with excellent food. However, it's not cheap once you add in the cinema tickets and the price of your meal.

H Jackie's Juice Bar

This lively little café in Denby Market is always busy because the salads and juices are really good for you and children love their home-made ice cream. Everything is made from the freshest ingredients available and it's great if you want a quick lunch.

Practice Test 2 • Reading

Part 3

For each question, choose the correct answer.

Kirsty Wade, age 19

I've always been keen on sport and very fit so a few years ago I decided to join my local athletics club. In the beginning I put all my effort into the long jump because it was my best event, but the coach encouraged me to try different things.

I ended up as a middle-distance runner, which means I don't run the short distances like 100 metres, or long cross-country races, but the in-between ones like 800 metres. It's an interesting type of running because you have to mix speed with strength. You also have to think a lot about how you race, and choose the right moment to run at your maximum speed. You need to do quite a lot of regular training when you first start and it helps if you have a good coach who can keep you motivated and teach you the basics.

I take part in some quite major competitions now, but I still remember my first race. I was so nervous before it started. And when it finished, I could still feel my hands shaking. It was a great race and I came second so I was very pleased. Since then I've learned to stay calm before and during races. I do a lot of breathing exercises that help me stay focused and relaxed. Competing has really helped me to trust in my own abilities. And now I find that I love running in front of a crowd – I suppose it's a sort of performance.

One thing I don't enjoy so much is how hard you have to work to stay fit and strong enough to race, although it helps that I often train with others. I try to eat and sleep well, but I don't have a special diet. Mostly it's a case of getting plenty of variety and eating more of everything because I'm so active.

I sometimes watch Olympic athletes on TV and imagine myself in their position. It must be a fantastic experience, but at the moment I don't feel that is necessarily where I'm aiming. I think you have to give up so much if you want to reach that level.

11 **Why did the writer join an athletics club?**

A Because she enjoyed taking part in sports.
B Because she thought she should get more exercise.
C Because she wanted to become an athletics coach.
D Because she wanted to become a professional long jumper.

12 **What does the writer say about 800-metre running?**

A You have to know when to run fastest.
B It's harder than running in the 100 metres.
C It's more important to be quick than strong.
D You need to forget everything and just run.

13 **What does the writer say about competing in races now?**

A It always makes her feel scared.
B It feels good to be in front during the race.
C It's helped her to develop new skills.
D She enjoys people watching her race.

14 **What does Kirsty say about the food she eats?**

A If she eats a lot, she can run faster.
B Eating plenty of food helps her to sleep better.
C She eats the same kind of things as other people.
D She would like to eat different types of food.

15 **Which best describes Kirsty?**

A A young athlete who trains hard and hopes to be selected for the Olympics in the future.

B A girl who was good at the long jump and likes running, but who doesn't see herself becoming an international athlete.

C A girl who's a keen athlete, but doesn't like running in front of a crowd and who finds the training very boring.

D A keen athlete who finds it enjoyable to practise with other people and compete as part of a team.

Practice Test 2 • Reading

Part 4

Five sentences have been removed from the text below.
For each question, choose the correct answer.
There are three extra sentences which you do not need to use.

Practice Test 2

A Helping Hand

Lee Newton was sitting on a station platform under an old blanket when he saw a young couple talking. **16** ________ It was a freezing night in January, and the couple were clearly cold. Lee called to them and asked them if they wanted to share his blanket. The three of them started chatting, and Lee learned that their names were Karen and Mark.

17 ________ Lee told them that he'd lost his job and then his flat when he could no longer pay the rent. He had no family to help him, and nowhere to go. **18** ________ Karen and Mark felt terrible. They couldn't imagine sleeping on the icy platform for even one night. As they spent their night in the station chatting to Lee, they realized that anyone could end up in his situation. **19** ________

When morning came, Karen and Mark bought an extra train ticket and invited Lee to come home with them. Lee accepted, and gratefully moved into Karen and Mark's spare bedroom. Once he had an address, Lee was able to apply for jobs. **20** ________ He saved up to buy a small motorbike, then got an evening job delivering pizzas. After a few months, Lee had saved up enough money to rent a small flat of his own.

'When times get tough, you need friends and family,' Lee says. 'Karen and Mark became that for me.' An act of kindness was all Lee needed to help him get his life back.

A He offered to drive them home.

B He'd been sleeping in the train station for three months.

C They'd missed the last train, and they seemed upset.

D They enjoyed living together, so Lee decided to stay.

E He soon found work in a local factory.

F They felt very lucky to have jobs and a home.

G It wasn't a big problem because he bought a flat.

H Karen explained that they lived two hours away and they couldn't afford a taxi home.

Practice Test 2 • Reading

Part 5

For each question, choose the correct answer.

Teenage Teachers

People may think teenagers are too young to be in charge of a class when they're still students themselves, but that's not true. Sixteen-year-olds are **21** ________ teaching lessons to primary school children in a new government scheme which allows school leavers to **22** ________ as teaching assistants in primary schools.

New rules were recently introduced which have allowed all primary school teachers to have more time during the school day for **23** ________ lessons, but this sometimes means that teachers have less time for teaching. Now teenagers fill the gap. They take a two-year course, starting when they're 14. When they enter the classroom as teachers **24** ________ than students, they have to quickly put into practice the skills they learned **25** ________ they were studying.

The government believes that about 18,000 teenagers could get jobs in this **26** ________. However, many people believe that young teenagers will not make suitable teachers.

	A	B	C	D
21	**A** currently	**B** newly	**C** previously	**D** recently
22	**A** be	**B** feel	**C** learn	**D** work
23	**A** practising	**B** preparing	**C** reading	**D** thinking
24	**A** even	**B** instead	**C** rather	**D** sooner
25	**A** except	**B** however	**C** throughout	**D** while
26	**A** kind	**B** style	**C** type	**D** way

Practice Test 2 • Writing

Part 2

Choose **one** of these questions.
Write your answer in about **100 words**.

Question 2

You see this notice on an English-language website.

> We need your articles!
>
> **FOOD**
> What kind of food do you like to eat?
> Do you prefer eating out or eating at home? Why?
> Write an article answering these questions and we will put it on our website!

Write your **article**.

Question 3

Your English teacher has asked you to write a story.
Your story must begin with this sentence:

When the postman gave me the parcel, I had no idea what was inside.

Write your **story**.

Practice Test 2 • Listening

Part 1

11 For each question, choose the correct answer.

1 What is the weather forecast for tomorrow?

A

B

C

2 What does Paul look like?

A

B

C

3 What exercise does the girl do at the moment?

A

B

C

4 What can teenagers do at the new club?

A

B

C

5 What equipment is missing?

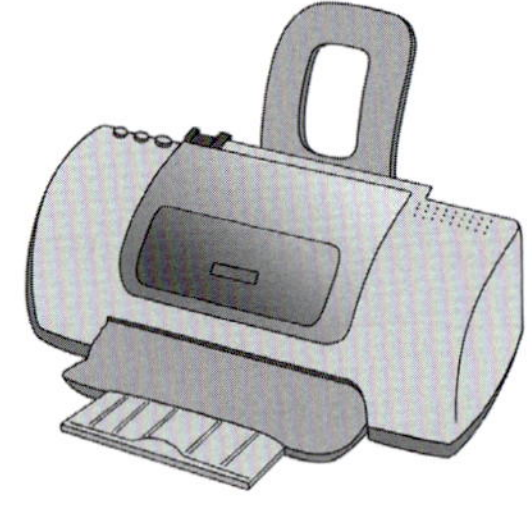

A B C

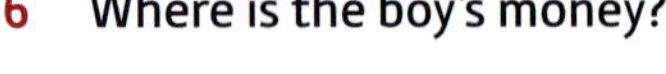

6 Where is the boy's money?

A B C

7 How did Susie contact her friend?

A B C

Practice Test 2 • Listening

Part 2

12 For each question, choose the correct answer.

8 You will hear two friends talking about a book they read.
The girl thinks that the book

A is too long.

B is not easy to understand.

C is worth reading again.

9 You will hear a man telling a friend about his neighbour.
The man thinks the neighbour

A has a lot of hobbies.

B is not very friendly.

C works very hard.

10 You will hear two people talking about a friend.
What do they say about him?

A He is always late.

B He likes expensive things.

C He didn't come last week.

11 You will hear two friends talking about a school trip.
The boy feels that

A there wasn't enough to see at the museum.

B the trip was too long.

C they didn't spend long enough at the museum.

Practice Test 2

12 **You will hear a woman telling a friend about her new home. How does she feel about it?**

A She thinks the neighbours are very noisy.

B She likes living in the city.

C She can't sleep in her new flat.

13 **You will hear two friends talking about a new supermarket. They think the supermarket would be better if**

A there were more people working there.

B there was a better selection of food.

C the prices were lower.

Practice Test 2 • Listening

Part 3

13 For each question, write the correct answer in the gap. Write **one** or **two words** or a **number** or a **date** or a **time**.

You will hear a travel expert talking about different holiday destinations.

HOLIDAY DESTINATIONS

The Canary Islands

Nice weather throughout the year.

La Gomera is a good place for **14** __________ .

Prices start at **15** __________ pounds each for a fortnight.

Sardinia

Variety of water sports available.

You can get a **16** __________ certificate.

Adults travelling with children cannot go in **17** __________ .

Iceland

Travel around Reykjavik on a **18** __________ .

Askja region has beautiful mountains.

Cost £1,200 – accommodation and **19** __________ are included in the price.

Practice Test 2 • Listening

Part 4

14 For each question, choose the correct answer.

You will hear someone talking about the Westbay Music Festival.

20 The first Westbay Festival
- **A** involved 12 bands.
- **B** took place in 1980.
- **C** lasted for one full day.

21 The festival
- **A** will attract a bigger crowd this year.
- **B** goes on for a whole weekend.
- **C** is aimed at adults and children.

22 The Big Smile Stage includes appearances by
- **A** local comedians only.
- **B** famous TV stars.
- **C** a top American entertainer.

23 What can you do inside the Big Blue Tent?
- **A** read the latest music biographies
- **B** watch thrillers on Saturday and Sunday nights
- **C** watch films about rock music

24 The presenter especially likes the fact that you can buy
- **A** unusual CDs.
- **B** outdoor clothes.
- **C** presents for other people.

25 What is special about the food at the festival?
- **A** The Mexican food is very hot.
- **B** There is more choice than at other events.
- **C** Everything is vegetarian.

Practice Test 2 • Speaking

Part 1

Phase 1: Select one or more questions from this list.

Personal details

- What's your name?
- What's your surname?
- How do you spell it?
- When's your birthday?
- Where are you from?
- Where do you work / study?

Phase 2: Select one or more questions from each of the following categories.

Where you live

- Where do you live?
- What activities can you do in your neighbourhood?
- What do you like about your neighbourhood?
- How can people travel around your town / city / area?

Free time

- Do you have any hobbies?
- What do you like doing after school?
- What activities do you enjoy doing on holiday?

Part 2

1 In a city
2 At work

Candidate A Look at the photo on page 210. It shows people in a city.
Say what you can see in the photo.

Candidate B Look at the photo on page 211. It shows people at work.
Say what you can see in the photo.

Practice Test 2 • Speaking

Parts 3 and 4

Free-time activities

Part 3

Two young people are planning to invite a few friends to their house this evening. They want to choose an activity which will be suitable for a group of people to take part in, and will help their friends to relax and have fun.

Here are some activities that they could do.

Talk together about the different activities, then decide which one would be best for a group of young people who want to relax and have fun.

Part 4

Answer and discuss together the following questions:

- What do you do in your free time?
- Which activities do you think are exciting / relaxing? Why?
- Which activities do you think are interesting / boring? Why?
- Which activities is it better to do alone / with someone else? Why?

BOOM

Practice Test 3 • Reading

Part 1

For each question, choose the correct answer.

1

Mobile phones are not permitted in this area.

Please go to reception or leave the building if you want to use your phone.

A It is forbidden to use a mobile phone in any part of this centre.

B You are allowed to use your mobile phone in one area of this centre.

C You can use the receptionist's phone if you need to make a call.

2

To: David
From: Aisha
Subject: Book

I'm really sorry I've lost the book you lent me. Where did you buy it? I'm going into town tomorrow and I'll get you another one.

Aisha wants David to

A lend her a book.

B go into town with her.

C give her the name of a shop.

3

Take this medicine
every six hours
on an empty stomach.

A You must eat six hours before you take this medicine.

B You can eat after you've taken this medicine.

C You need to have this medicine six times a day.

4

These changing rooms are for people having tennis lessons.

If you are not having lessons, please use the main changing room.

The Manager

A You can only use the main changing room if you are having lessons.

B Only leisure centre staff are allowed in these changing rooms.

C These changing rooms are for people learning to play tennis.

5

Please switch off the lights when you leave.

The security guard will lock the doors when you have left.

A You must lock the doors and turn off the lights when you go home.

B You must ask the security guard to let you turn off the lights.

C The security guard doesn't usually turn off the lights in this building.

5 How did Ben find the information for his article?

A

B

C

6 Where did the man leave the passports?

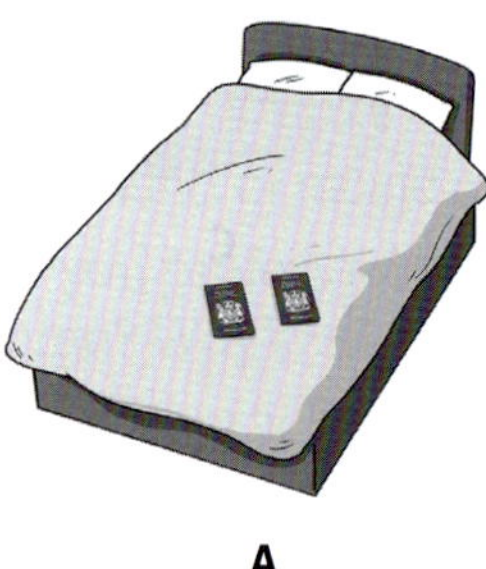

A

B

C

7 Where is the woman going?

A

B

C

Practice Test 3 • Listening

Part 2

16 For each question, choose the correct answer.

8 You will hear two friends talking about a play.
What do they say about it?

A It was much better than they thought it would be.

B It went on for too long.

C The actors forgot what they were supposed to say.

9 You will hear a man telling a friend about his new phone.
What does he say about it?

A He finds it difficult to type messages on it.

B He can't take good photos with it.

C He can't get all his favourite apps on it.

10 You will hear two people talking about a train.
What does the woman say about it?

A It'll be here in another ten minutes.

B It's been involved in an accident.

C It won't be arriving at the station.

11 You will hear two friends talking about a restaurant.
The woman thinks that

A they are going to be late to meet their friends.

B their booking is later than she would have liked.

C the food is not as good as she had hoped.

12 You will hear two people talking about a newspaper.
The woman thinks the newspaper

A is good value for money.

B does not print accurate information.

C is very old-fashioned.

13 You will hear a woman telling a friend about her holiday.
How does she feel about it?

A It was a bit boring.

B It made her feel very tired.

C It was nice and relaxing.

Practice Test 3 • Listening

Part 3

17 For each question, write the correct answer in the gap. Write **one** or **two words** or a **number** or a **date** or a **time**.

You will hear a woman talking about a conference.

Toy Sale Conference

9.30-10.00: **14** __________ to the conference by Sally Connor

10.00–11.00: *Our Company in Tokyo* – a talk by Kenji Nakamura followed by a short film

11.00–11.30: Half an hour for **15** __________

Buffet lunch in Victoria Hall – **16** __________ the library

2.00–3.30: *Toys in Britain: Success and Failure* – a talk by Robert Price (owner of over **17** __________ toy shops)

3.30–5.00: *What's Next for Toys?* – a talk by Sarah Smith, Sales **18** __________

19 __________ in the Green Room (1st floor)

Practice Test 3

Practice Test 4 • Speaking

Parts 3 and 4

Choosing a present

Part 3

A young man is planning to buy a present for his younger sister, but he isn't sure what to buy. He hasn't got very much money, but he wants to get her something she will like.

Here are some possible presents he could choose.

Talk together about the different presents, then decide which one would be best for the young man's sister.

Part 4

Answer and discuss together the following questions:

- How often do you buy people presents?
- What kinds of presents do you like to give?
- What kinds of presents to you like to get?
- How do you feel when someone gives you a present?

12:30

Practice Test 5 • Reading

Part 1

For each question, choose the correct answer.

1

Evening Art Classes

If you wish to do art classes next month, go to Room 58 and tell Paul Davidson (the art teacher) by 30th April.

A You must say if you want to study art before the end of April.

B The art class will be in Room 58 from the end of April.

C You should give your art work to Mr Davidson in Room 58.

2

Ruby

Michael

Please ask Dave to wait for me at the airport, not the train station in town. His plane lands at 11.30 p.m. but the last train leaves from the airport at 10.45 p.m.

Ruby should

A take Michael and Dave to the airport this evening.

B ask Dave to take the train that leaves at 10.45 p.m.

C tell Dave to meet Michael at the airport instead of the station.

3

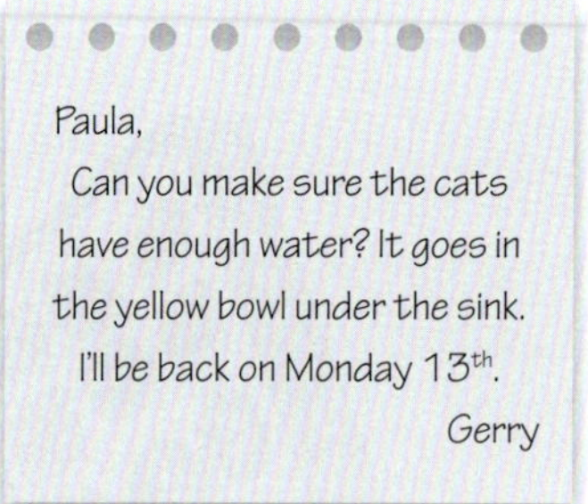

Paula,

Can you make sure the cats have enough water? It goes in the yellow bowl under the sink. I'll be back on Monday 13th.

Gerry

Gerry is asking Paula to

A check his pets when she returns on Monday.

B buy a yellow bowl to use for the cats' water.

C give his pets something to drink while he's away.

4

ATTENTION!

Long vehicles may be turning ahead.
Do not park near the crossroads.

A Drivers should be careful where they leave their cars.

B Large lorries must not park on the corner of the road.

C Cars should not be parked too close to each other.

5

Purse containing photos and several banknotes found in shop.

Call manager on **08081 570987**.

A The owner of a lost wallet has left their contact number in a shop.

B Someone's money and pictures were lost in a shop.

C The shop manager has taken some pictures.

Practice Test 5

Practice Test 5 • Reading

Part 3

For each question, choose the correct answer.

Buddy Jones, musician

I'm a session musician, which means that people hire me when they need a musician, rather than me working for a particular band or on my own. It's still important to me that I'm doing what I like and believe in, so I don't accept all the work I'm offered. I've been doing this job for quite some time and I'm happy to consider the offers and then decide.

You need certain qualities to be a good session musician. One such quality is that you have to be able to fit quickly into a team. It's no good if you go to the studio and have an argument with the trumpet player. It helps if you get along with people you've just met, as very often you play with musicians you've never seen before. Then of course there are particular musical skills you need. For example, you've got to learn parts very quickly and be able to play a lot of different musical styles. And of course, despite all your talents, you are in the background, so you have to be prepared to let somebody else be admired.

Another very important quality that you definitely need to have is flexibility. Some bands may have rehearsals at specific times and you need to be there when they need you. Sometimes a band or a solo artist may call you for a recording at the last minute because a musician hasn't turned up, and it's important that you can be there at short notice.

I've found there's plenty of variety in this work. Sometimes I'm asked to play guitar for a top band at a big live concert. Or I might go on a long tour with a famous singer. But my main income has always been from studio work. I might do one short section of a song, or I could be asked to join a band for a whole album.

Most session musicians generally get paid the same amount. It's fairly good money, but of course if an album I work on sells a million copies, the band make a huge amount of money, but nobody gives me a big cheque.

11 What does Buddy say that a session musician does?

A pays other musicians to work with him/her
B makes money with his/her own band
C earns money performing alone
D works for different bands for a payment

12 According to Buddy, what makes a good session musician?

A someone who's willing to spend a lot of time learning
B someone who can play many types of music
C someone who admires many famous musicians
D someone who's flexible about attending long rehearsals

13 What does Buddy say about his job?

A He doesn't like being away from home.
B He'd like to record his own album one day.
C He rarely gets to work with famous musicians.
D He gets to do a lot of different things.

14 What does Buddy say about his pay?

A He gets paid extra if an album does well.
B Most of it comes from making recordings.
C He usually gets a large cheque when he's finished.
D Different session musicians get different amounts of money.

15 What might Buddy say about his life as a musician?

A I like my job because I get to do a lot of different things in music and I'm not worried about being famous.

B I'm good at my job because I like entertaining people and appearing on television.

C I love being a musician because I get a chance to meet famous people and earn a lot of money.

D I enjoy my job because I get the chance to play a lot of instruments and try out different types of music.

Practice Test 5

Practice Test 5 • Reading

Part 4

Five sentences have been removed from the text below.
For each question, choose the correct answer.
There are three extra sentences which you do not need to use.

Saved by dolphins

I've always loved the sea, and I started surfing when I was five years old. I live near the beach in California, so I try to get out on the waves every day.

16 ________ It was a warm, windy day with some good waves. I was resting on my board and watching a group of bottlenose dolphins playing in the surf a short distance away, when suddenly a great white shark appeared. It was huge, but it moved so fast that I didn't see it coming.

The shark tried to bite me, but it couldn't get its teeth around me and the board. It tore a big chunk out of the board, but I wasn't hurt that time. Then the shark came at me again. **17** ________ I was terrified and my leg was bleeding, but I tried to paddle away, knowing that the next bite was seconds away. **18** ________ I looked up and saw the bottlenose dolphins swimming around me. They formed a circle around me and my surfboard, so the shark couldn't get near me. I was amazed. It was like something out of a film.

I knew a lot of stories about dolphins helping humans, but I never really believed them until it happened to me. Dolphins are very intelligent and they knew what to do to help me stay safe. They stayed close to me until I managed to get back on my board and catch a wave back to the shore, where I collapsed with relief. Someone who was at the beach called an ambulance, and I was taken to hospital.

19 ________ I won't give up my favourite activity. I'm not angry with the shark.
20 ________ I'll always be grateful to the dolphins. They saved my life.

Practice Test 5

A I've stayed out of the sea ever since.

B But the next bite never came.

C Six weeks later, I was back on my surfboard.

D Two months ago, I went surfing alone.

E I've always loved dolphins.

F I know I was in his home, and he was protecting it.

G I knew that I would survive the attack.

H This time it bit my leg and pulled me off my surfboard.

Practice Test 5 • Reading

Part 5

For each question, choose the correct answer.

Healthy snacks on the run

In today's busy lives we often have little time for healthy eating, so we do the easy thing and eat snacks like crisps or sweets instead. **21** ________, it's possible to eat quickly and healthily. All you **22** ________ to do is to follow a few simple rules.

First of all, read what it **23** ________ on the packet before you buy a snack. This is important because people often think that they're buying healthy snacks, but sugar may be the **24** ________ ingredient.

Try to look for healthier options – instead of eating ice cream, try frozen fruit juices and, most importantly, eat at **25** ________ times of the day. Learn when your body needs food so **26** ________ you don't suddenly feel the need to eat a lot of unhealthy snack food.

	A	B	C	D
21	**A** Ago	**B** Alike	**C** However	**D** Whenever
22	**A** can	**B** must	**C** need	**D** should
23	**A** puts	**B** says	**C** talks	**D** writes
24	**A** big	**B** great	**C** large	**D** main
25	**A** common	**B** equal	**C** even	**D** regular
26	**A** that	**B** what	**C** when	**D** which

Practice Test 5 • Reading

Part 6

For each question, write the correct answer.
Write **one** word for each gap.

If you ever visit the USA, don't miss the chance to visit the Smithsonian Institute. It's made up of 17 museums and galleries and the National Zoo in Washington D.C., as **27** ________ as two museums in New York City.

The Smithsonian museums feature exhibits related **28** ________ art, design, technology, history and culture, and contain about 154 million objects. You can learn **29** ________ everything from the origins of man at the Natural History Museum to the future of space travel at the Air and Space Museum.

If you spent one minute at each exhibit, it would take **30** ________ than 258 years to see them all.

Best of **31** ________, it's free to enter all the Smithsonian museums and galleries, so you can learn about anything in the world **32** ________ paying a penny!

Practice Test 5

Practice Test 5 • Writing

Part 1

You **must** answer this question.
Write your answer in about **100 words**.

Question 1

Read this email from your English-speaking friend Peter and the notes you have made.

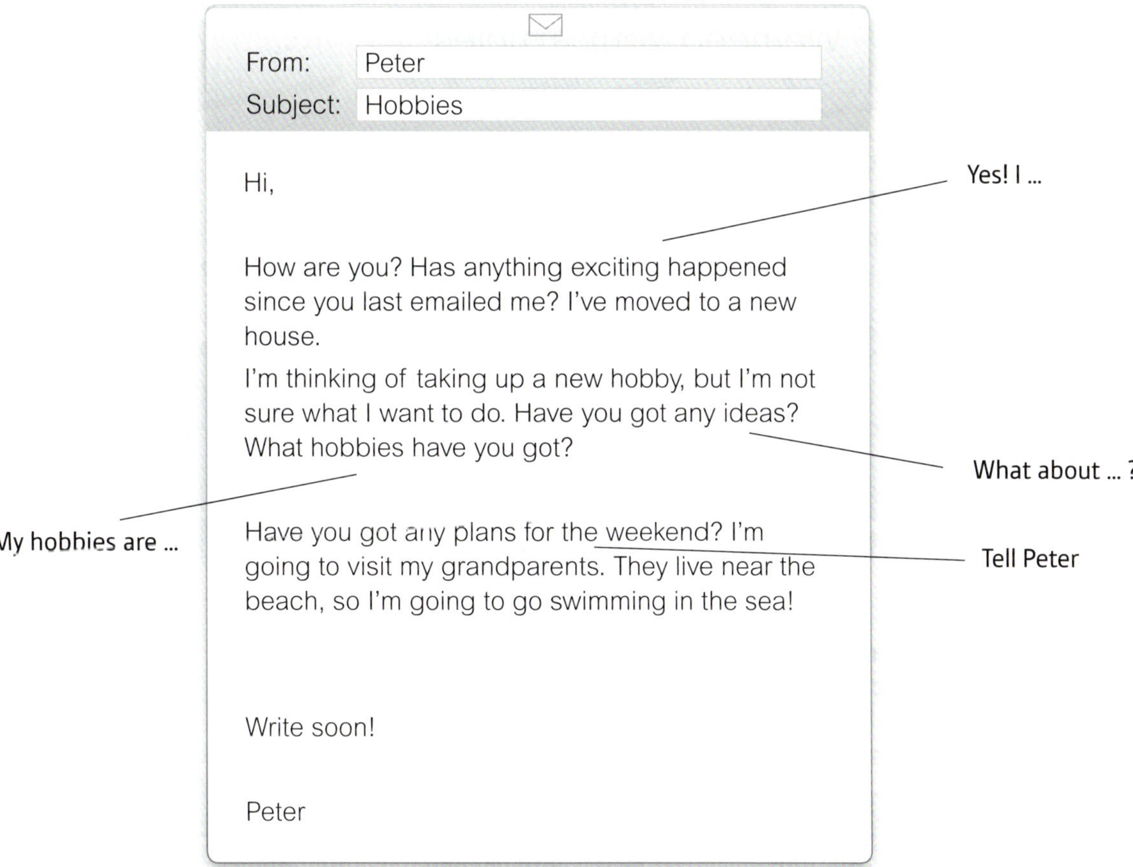

From: Peter
Subject: Hobbies

Hi,

How are you? Has anything exciting happened since you last emailed me? I've moved to a new house.

I'm thinking of taking up a new hobby, but I'm not sure what I want to do. Have you got any ideas? What hobbies have you got?

Have you got any plans for the weekend? I'm going to visit my grandparents. They live near the beach, so I'm going to go swimming in the sea!

Write soon!

Peter

Write your **email** to Peter using **all the notes**.

Practice Test 5

Practice Test 5 • Speaking

Parts 3 and 4

Travelling around Europe

Part 3

Three of your friends want to travel around Europe by train. They are trying to decide what things they need to take with them. They don't want to carry too much.

Here are some things which they could take with them.

Talk together about the things they will need. Decide which two things are the most important to take with them.

Part 4

Answer and discuss together the following questions:

- Do you enjoy travelling? Why (not)?
- What other countries have you visited?
- What other countries would you like to visit? Why?
- What's the best way to travel to / around other countries? Why?

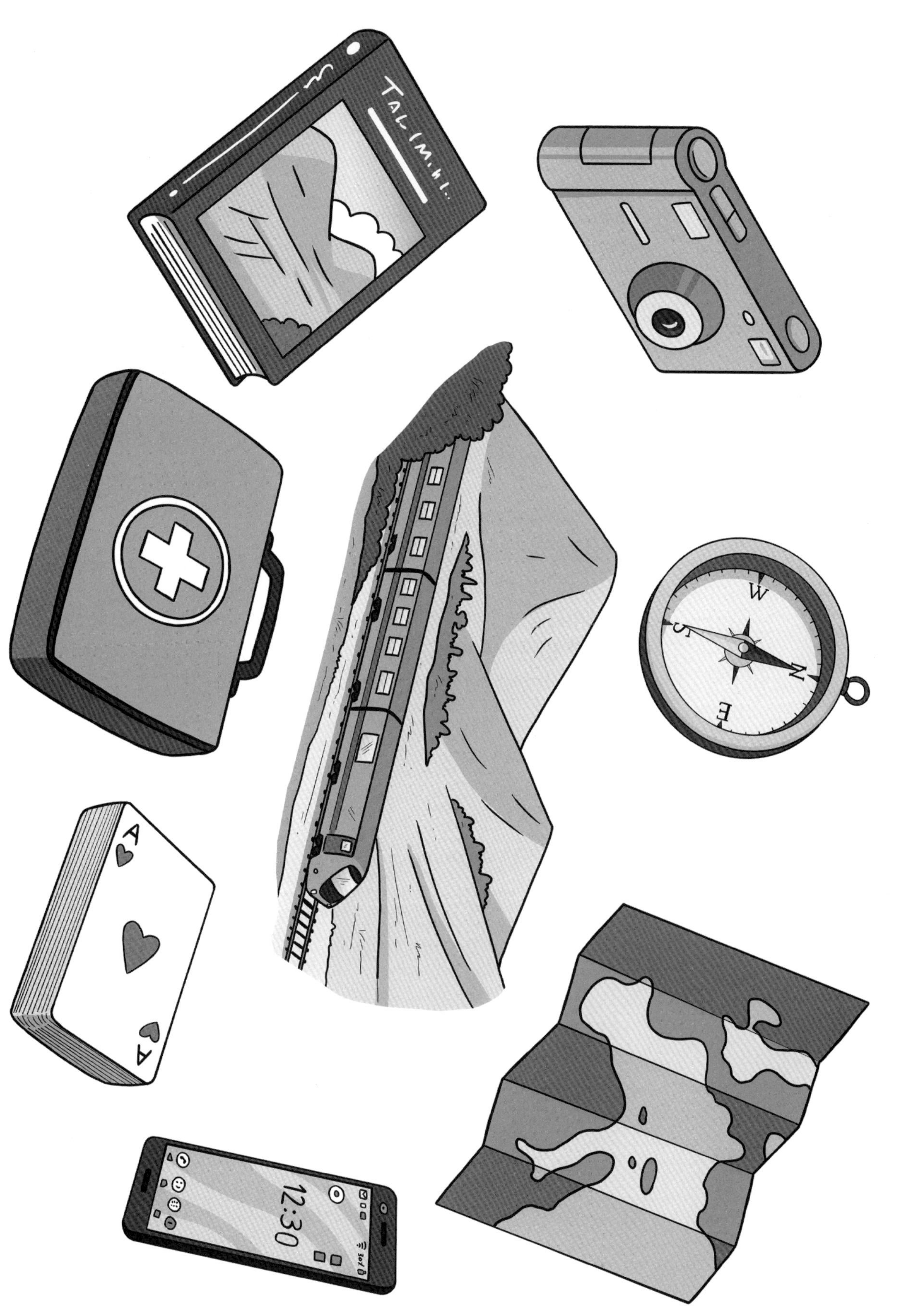

Practice Test 5

Practice Test 6 • Reading

Part 1

For each question, choose the correct answer.

1

Spaces are available on our climbing and diving courses.

Please ask at reception for full details.

A This leisure centre needs a new receptionist.

B All the courses at this centre are full.

C The receptionist will give you information about courses.

2

CUSTOMER NOTICE

These stairs are to be used for emergency purposes only.

A Only the emergency services can use these stairs.

B Customers are never allowed to use these stairs.

C Anybody can use these stairs if there is an emergency.

3

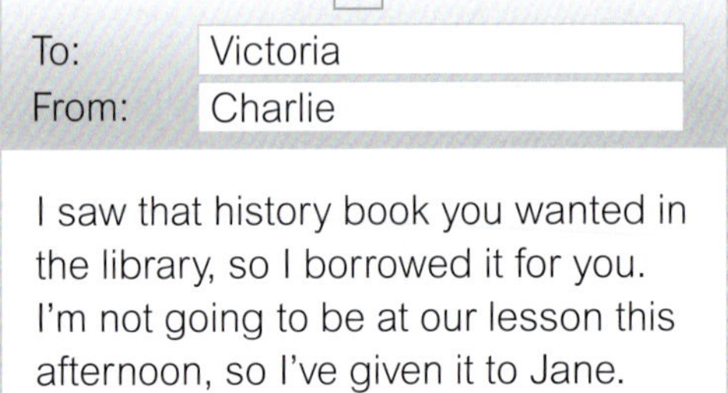

To: Victoria
From: Charlie

I saw that history book you wanted in the library, so I borrowed it for you. I'm not going to be at our lesson this afternoon, so I've given it to Jane.

A Jane is going to give Victoria a book today.

B Charlie needs the history book this afternoon.

C This afternoon's history lesson is cancelled.

4

We're getting new lockers in the gym. If you'd like one, but you haven't reserved one yet, you should see me before Friday.

Jan Harper

A It's still possible to have a new locker.

B You will be able to use your new locker on Friday.

C New lockers can be reserved from Friday.

5

Isabel,
Sam can't be at the meeting until ten o'clock today. Please start without him.

A Sam wants to change the day of the meeting.

B Sam is going to be late for the meeting.

C The meeting is going to start later than planned.

Practice Test 6 • Reading

Part 2

For each question, choose the correct answer.

The people below want to buy a magazine.
On the opposite page there are descriptions of eight magazines.
Decide which magazine would be the most suitable for the people below.

6 

Lynn has a flat in the city and is always looking for new places to go where she lives. She wants a magazine that will give her some ideas. She likes going out in the evenings and she's keen on cultural events.

7 

Tom is interested in watching unusual and exciting sports. He would like to buy a magazine that will recommend the best events in his area. He would also like to get an idea of ticket costs for the events.

8 

Jack and Hannah are thinking of giving up their jobs and starting their own business abroad. They like to read about other people's experiences. They would like to read about the advantages and disadvantages of moving abroad and also to get useful tips on how best to do it.

9 

Maria enjoys reading about celebrities. She likes looking at pictures of actors and pop artists at special events and in their own homes. She enjoys looking at their outfits and new fashions.

10 

Ben and Maggie like to read about what's going on in the world today. They prefer real stories about political events. They like reading interesting articles about current affairs.

THE BEST MAGAZINES FOR YOU

A What, Where, How?

Although we have regular articles on farming and animals, our magazine is full of information for city visitors who are interested in pretty villages, long walks and good restaurants and pubs. If you're planning a weekend in the countryside, get your copy of *What, Where, How?*, special discount vouchers for many local cafés and everything you need to know to have a great weekend away.

B Starter

Read about the real experiences of motocross riders, skydivers, and rock climbers in the latest edition of *Starter*. We also have a full guide to all the best competitions and other activities going on across Britain this month. Special section with everything you need to know for each sports event, venue, prices and much more.

C Score

Score is more than just a football magazine. We also have articles about other popular sports including basketball and motor racing, and interviews with top athletes. This week's star article is on American football. It features one of the best all time stars in the history of American football.

D Focus

Focus is a serious magazine that deals with serious stories in the news today. All our articles and interviews are lively and intelligent and written by experienced journalists. Subscribe for our three-month offer and get one old issue for free.

E New Perspectives

This month we talk to three couples who have changed their lives by moving somewhere completely new. There's also a special article giving advice to other people who are thinking about doing the same. Packed with practical ideas so that your move goes smoothly.

F Review

Find out about the latest Hollywood films, the best theatres and the most original art galleries in *Review* magazine. Interesting articles and great photography makes this the best review magazine around. Special section with art gallery listings and theatre reviews.

G Update

Find out what's on by looking through *Update* magazine. We list all events from clubs, pubs, leisure centres, cinemas, restaurants and a lot more so you can do more with your money. It includes listings for all areas of the city for events for next month. Get *Update* and you will never miss an event again.

H Sparkles

We have the best photos, the best stories and the most interesting news about all your favourite stars. This month, look out for a top interview with one of the biggest names in entertainment. What they're up to, what they wear and their latest favourite trends are all in *Sparkles*.

Practice Test 6 • Reading

Part 4

Five sentences have been removed from the text below.
For each question, choose the correct answer.
There are three extra sentences which you do not need to use.

My first marathon

The alarm went off at half past four that morning. It was far too early to get up, and the idea of running 26 miles seemed impossible. **16** ________ I pulled myself out of bed, showered and pulled on my running gear.

By six o'clock, I was at the Dodger Stadium, where the rest of my running group was already waiting. When they saw the look of terror on my face, they laughed kindly. This was clearly my first marathon. **17** ________ When I realized that I was just one of them, I felt a little better. Helicopters hovered overhead ready to film us as we ran through the streets of Los Angeles, passing every major landmark until we reached the sea at Santa Monica. Suddenly, I felt very lucky and proud to be a part of it. **18** ________

As I began to run, I tried to ignore the aches in my body from eight months of training. Instead, I put one foot in front of the other and kept going. By mile five, my body was complaining, and by mile eight, my muscles were screaming at me.

19 ________ I was running alone now, but I was still running. By mile 12, I was ready to give up, and by mile 15, I was moving even more slowly. By mile 18, I was in my neighbourhood. **20** ________ But by mile 22, there were only four miles to go. Spectators yelled encouragement at me as I ran past. 'You can do it! Keep going!'

As the finish line came into sight, I started running faster and faster, and I crossed that line running. I grinned as the medal was placed over my head, and then I cried. I had done it. I had run my first marathon!

A After eight months of training, this was going to be easy.

B I slowed down, and the rest of my group moved away.

C But I had trained for this, and I was going to do it.

D There was no way I could finish the race now.

E The horn blew to start the race.

F I was very tempted to turn down my street and go home.

G I was so glad that I had decided to do this.

H Thousands of runners from all over the world were gathered for the race.

Practice Test 6

Practice Test 6 • Reading

Part 5

For each question, choose the correct answer.

Stay Healthy by Walking

Everybody worries about their general health and fitness. However, what many people don't realize is that walking is one of the best ways to keep healthy.

This doesn't mean that you **21** __________ to go on long walks in the countryside. You can walk home from work or school. You can walk to the shops. You can use the stairs **22** __________ of using the lift. You can even walk a dog **23** __________ you have one!

Now let's look **24** __________ the benefits of walking. Firstly, it's relaxing. Secondly, it improves your fitness and your health. **25** __________, it's a great way to socialize with your friends and family.

Remember, you don't need **26** __________ expensive equipment for walking. You just need a good pair of walking boots or shoes.

	A	B	C	D
21	**A** must	**B** have	**C** should	**D** might
22	**A** instead	**B** enough	**C** else	**D** well
23	**A** whether	**B** if	**C** as	**D** that
24	**A** on	**B** at	**C** for	**D** with
25	**A** Finally	**B** Conclusion	**C** End	**D** Last
26	**A** many	**B** any	**C** various	**D** some

Practice Test 6

Practice Test 6 • Reading

Part 6

For each question, write the correct answer.
Write **one** word for each gap.

My friends and I have started a book club, and we'd love it if you decided to join us. We choose one book to read every week, and then we meet up at **27** __________ end of the week to discuss the book.

We meet every Thursday, at a different club member's house each week. The host for each week provides drinks and a **28** __________ snacks.

We share our thoughts and ideas **29** __________ the books, and we usually chat about a lot of other topics, too! It's a great way to **30** __________ to know people and to find **31** __________ about some interesting books.

If you'd like to join the book club, let me know, and I'll **32** __________ you what book we decide to read next!

Practice Test 6

Practice Test 6 • Writing

Part 1

You **must** answer this question.
Write your answer in about **100 words**.

Question 1

Read this email from your English-speaking friend Gina and the notes you have made.

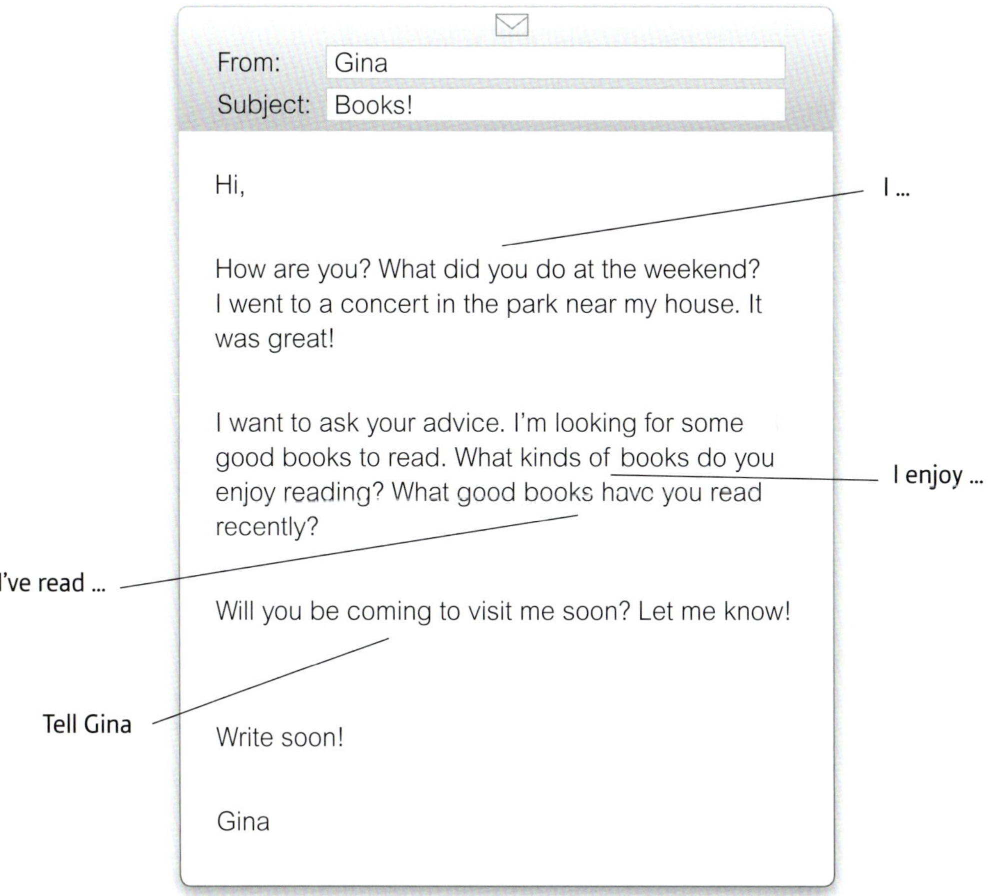
From: Gina
Subject: Books!

Hi,

How are you? What did you do at the weekend? I went to a concert in the park near my house. It was great!

I want to ask your advice. I'm looking for some good books to read. What kinds of books do you enjoy reading? What good books have you read recently?

Will you be coming to visit me soon? Let me know!

Write soon!

Gina

Write your **email** to Gina using **all the notes**.

Practice Test 6

Practice Test 6 • Writing

Part 2

Choose **one** of these questions.
Write your answer in about **100 words**.

Question 2

You see this notice on an English-language website.

> We need your articles!
>
> KEEPING FIT
>
> Is it important to keep fit? Why?
>
> What's the best way to keep fit?
>
> How do you keep fit?
>
> Write an article answering these questions and we will put it on our website!

Write your **article**.

Question 3

Your English teacher has asked you to write a story.
Your story must begin with this sentence:

It was the worst journey I had ever been on.

Write your **story**.

Practice Test 6 • Listening

Part 1

27 For each question, choose the correct answer.

1 What is the woman going to buy today?

A

B

C

2 What time did Sarah finish work today?

A

B

C

3 What is the woman planning to do at the weekend?

A

B

C

4 What is the weather going to be like this afternoon?

A

B

C

Practice Test 6

5 How did the man find out about the play?

A B C

6 When is the man's first guitar lesson?

A B C

7 How does the woman usually keep fit?

A B C

Practice Test 6 • Listening

Part 2

28 For each question, choose the correct answer.

8 You will hear two people talking about the weather.
What does the man say?

A He doesn't think weather forecasts are accurate.
B He enjoys wet weather.
C He trusts the weather app he uses.

9 You will hear a woman telling a friend about her dreams.
What does she say?

A She wants to continue working in the city.
B She thinks she could make a lot of money as an artist.
C She doesn't think her dream is possible at the moment.

10 You will hear two friends talking about a trip.
What do they decide to do?

A Leave their car at the airport while they are on holiday.
B Ask David to take them to the airport in his car.
C Take a train to the airport.

11 You will hear a man telling a friend about his job.
What does he say about it?

A He has to stay in good physical condition.
B He is in dangerous situations every day.
C He doesn't get on very well with the rest of his team.

12 **You will hear two people talking about a supermarket.**
What does the woman say?

A She doesn't like buying clothes for her family there.

B The shop doesn't sell all the things she needs.

C She doesn't like it when the products get moved to new places.

13 **You will hear two friends talking about a computer game.**
What does the girl say about it?

A The story is a bit boring.

B The characters look very realistic.

C The puzzles are very easy.

Practice Test 6 • Listening

Part 3

29 For each question, write the correct answer in the gap. Write **one** or **two words** or a **number** or a **date** or a **time**.

You will hear a woman talking to a group of tourists about their holiday.

Greek Holidays

Meals

Meals will be served in the dining room which is located at the **14** __________ of the hotel.

Breakfast **15** __________ a.m.–9 a.m.

Lunch 12 p.m.–3 p.m.

Dinner 8 p.m.–11 p.m. (includes traditional **16** __________ twice a week).

Activities

Mornings

Trips include visits to **17** __________ ruins and monuments.

Visit to an outdoor market every **18** __________ .

Afternoons

Visit the beach (only **19** __________ away).

Stay by the hotel swimming pool.

Practice Test 6

Practice Test 6 • Listening

Part 4

30 For each question, choose the correct answer.

You will hear an interview with the manager of a new leisure centre.

20 Why is the leisure centre already so popular?

A It's the only leisure centre in the area.
B People have heard a lot about it.
C It has an excellent gym.

21 What will be added to the leisure centre soon?

A two new swimming pools
B a diving area
C a pool for children

22 The manager wants to improve the gym by

A buying more equipment.
B employing more staff.
C opening for more hours.

23 From next week, there will be

A an outdoor basketball court.
B a new court for volleyball.
C more tennis courts.

24 Who gives the scuba-diving lessons?

A a swimming instructor from the leisure centre
B instructors from a local diving school
C the manager himself

25 What is different about the leisure centre?

A The café sells healthy food.
B It's cheaper than most other centres.
C It offers discounts.

Audioscripts

Preparation & Practice Test 1

Listening

Part 1 Preparation

01

1 **Woman** I eat a lot of fruit and vegetables because they're good for me. I have a salad every day. Even though pizza is what I like the most, I only eat it once a week. Pizza isn't a very healthy food!

2 **Boy** The concert was amazing, wasn't it? Most of the songs were brilliant.

Girl Yeah, and I'm glad they played their hit song first. It's so cheerful.

Boy I was surprised by the final one, though. It was kind of strange.

Girl You're right. It wasn't really typical of their style.

3 **Boy** Hi Tom, it's Faisal. My tennis lesson was just starting when you rang at 10.30. Sorry I missed you. I'm so tired now; the lesson didn't end until 12.00! Hey, can you call me back around 2.15 if you have time?

4 **Woman** I'm taking a trip to Spain next week. Does your sister, Elena, still live there?

Man No, she's living in Italy at the moment. She used to live in Madrid, though.

Part 1 Practice

02

1 **When will the wedding take place?**

Woman Are you going to Mike's party on the 14th?
Man I'm not sure if I'll be here or not. You see, I'm travelling to Edinburgh on the 15th for my brother's wedding and the train leaves early in the morning. I don't want to be tired after a late night. My brother's not actually getting married until the 17th, but I want to spend a bit of time in Edinburgh before the wedding.

2 **What is the woman going to buy today?**

Man Can you get some milk and some butter when you go to the shop, please? I want to do some cooking later.

Woman We don't need any milk; I bought some yesterday. It's in the fridge, on the bottom shelf. I'll just get butter and bread.

Man We've got plenty of bread. I went to the new bakery on the corner this morning. Don't buy any more.

3 **What is the man going to do on Saturday?**

Woman I'm going to the cinema on Saturday afternoon. Do you want to come with me? There's a new comedy film playing, and it looks great.

Man I'd love to, but I need to go shopping. I must buy my mother a birthday present. It's her 60th birthday party on Sunday.

Woman Well, why don't you go shopping this evening instead? Then you can come to the cinema.

Man OK. That's a good idea. I'll do that.

4 **What did the woman do last Sunday?**

Man I went to the beach with my family last weekend. I had a great time.

Woman But it rained, didn't it? I remember, because we were having a picnic in the park and we had to run home with all our things. We got soaked!

Man That was on Saturday. We went on Sunday when it was nice and sunny.

Woman Oh yes, you're right. I remember now. I sat in the garden all day.

5 **How did the man book his holiday?**

Man I've booked a fantastic holiday in Italy for next month. I can't wait to go!

Woman That sounds exciting. I'd love to go to Italy. Did you book it on the Internet?

Man No, I don't like booking things on the Internet. I phoned the travel agent, told her what I wanted and she found me just the right thing. I'm going there to pick up the tickets next week.

6 **What time is the exam?**

Girl Why aren't you ready to go? It's nearly one o'clock. We need to hurry if we're going to get to the exam hall in time. The traffic is really bad today.

Boy What's the rush? The exam's not until 4.00.

Girl No, it starts at 2.00 and ends at 4.00. Check your exam timetable!

Boy Really? Oh no! How did I get that wrong? We'd better hurry up, then! I'll just grab my things.

7 **Why are there delays on the road?**

Woman Now for the latest traffic and travel news. There are delays on the A60 between Nottingham and Mansfield as a result of the recent weather conditions. Although the heavy rain did not have much effect on the speed of the traffic, a fallen tree now means that police have made the decision to close a section of the road. Luckily, traffic is still fairly light on the surrounding routes and the road should be open again before people start returning home from work.

Part 2 Preparation

03

1 **Girl** That was the worst exam ever! I wasn't able to finish any of the questions.

Boy Oh, sorry to hear that. But, if you don't mind my saying, it seemed fair enough to me, actually. I mean, all the topics we studied came up ...

Audioscripts

Girl Yeah, I probably should have revised more. Parts of it were so complicated, though.

Boy Look, don't worry too much. I'm sure you're going to get a good grade.

Girl I doubt it. But thanks!

2 **Man** Fantastic news: my football team has just bought the top player in the world.

Woman Sorry, I think it's disgusting to pay anyone so much money.

Man Oh, come on. That's just the way it works in premier league football. You know that.

Woman Doesn't make it right. So, one man is paid millions to kick a ball while people all over the world have nothing to eat ... how is that a good thing?

Man Well, I accept that a lot of people have no money for food, but many of the players do loads of work for charity.

Woman It's not enough! I can't believe you're defending this. It doesn't make sense.

3 **Woman** The new restaurant on Green Street is amazing, isn't it?

Man Well, I think it's pretty good, but I wouldn't call it amazing.

Woman Really?

Man Yeah, I had an excellent burger, but the desserts were disappointing.

Woman What did you think of the atmosphere?

Man Too noisy for me, I'm afraid! The waiters couldn't have been better, though, and the prices were fair.

Part 2 Practice

04

8 You will hear two friends talking about a singer.

Man Have you heard Kaylee's new song?

Woman Yes, I heard it last night. Do you like it?

Man It's good, but I prefer her earlier songs. Her last album was amazing.

Woman I agree with you. I read an interview with her and she said that she's been working with a songwriter lately. They've written the lyrics and music for her new album together. I think she produces better music when she writes her own songs. She's got real talent, and she's very creative.

Man She's got a great voice, too.

9 You will hear two friends talking about a new café.

Man I haven't been to this café before.

Woman Nor have I. It's only been open for a few weeks.

Man The food is delicious, isn't it?

Woman It's lovely. And the staff are really friendly, too.

Man Yes, they're very cheerful and polite. They described all the dishes on the menu to help us order.

Woman I know! Well, some of the dishes do have funny names, so it's good to know what they are! I just wish the seats weren't so uncomfortable.

Man I know what you mean. These chairs are very hard.

10 You will hear a woman telling a friend about her new job.

Man Are you enjoying your new job?

Woman Yes, I am. Well, most of the time, anyway.

Man Oh?

Woman The people I work with are very nice, and the boss isn't too bad. I do find the work interesting, and it's nice to be part of a team. I just find the hours a bit much. I start at eight in the morning, which is much earlier than I'm used to. It means that I have to get up at six to get to work on time. Some days I struggle to stay awake until home time!

Man Oh dear! You should talk to your boss.

11 You will hear two friends talking about their teacher.

Girl I wish we didn't have Mr Harris teaching us history.

Boy Why? Don't you like him?

Girl It's not that. He's a good teacher, and he always explains things really well. He makes the lessons interesting and easy to understand, which is really good.

Boy I know. I never used to like history before, but I really enjoy lessons with Mr Harris.

Girl Me too. But I wish he wouldn't give us so much homework on a Friday. Now I've got to spend the whole weekend studying!

Boy No, you haven't! We'll go to the library together this evening and we'll be finished in time to enjoy the weekend!

12 You will hear two friends talking about a film they watched.

Man Well, that was disappointing.

Woman Didn't you enjoy it? I laughed all the way through! There were some fantastic lines in that film. I wish I could remember them all!

Man It was funny, I'll admit that. But I was expecting there to be a bit more action, to be honest. The trailer we saw last week made the film look really exciting.

Woman That's true. It was more of a comedy than an adventure film. But at least it had a great cast. You have to admit that the acting was brilliant.

Man Yeah. I suppose so.

13 You will hear two friends talking about a website they use.

Girl I see they've updated Chatter again.

Boy I know! I wish they wouldn't do that. Every time I get used to using it, they change it again.

Girl Yes, but they always improve it and add cool new features. Look, now you can have private group chats with your friends. And you can add videos to your posts.

Boy Hmm. But now I can't find my photo albums. Have all my photos disappeared?

Girl Don't panic. You haven't lost them. They're just here, under Photo Options.

Boy Oh, right.

Girl You'll get the hang of it soon!

Part 3 Preparation

05

1 **Man** Freya was born in 1979 and she lived in Scotland until 1991. Her family moved to Spain and they lived there for four years. When they left Madrid in 1995, she was 16 years old.

2 **Woman** The cottage is available to rent on a weekly basis from June until September. In December, it can be rented for a maximum two-night stay.

3 **Man** The speech will begin at 11.00 a.m. but members of the public are asked to take their seats by 10.45. Doors will be open from 10.30.

4 **Woman** You can plant carrots in rows that should be around 30 centimetres apart. Don't plant them deeper than two centimetres in the ground. Remember to keep the plants around seven centimetres apart.

5 **Man** The bookshop is around the corner from the town hall. It's on Wingate Street opposite the vegetarian café. You'll see the big sculpture of a fish beside it.

Part 3 Practice

06

You will hear a man talking to a class of students about a language course.

Man Hello, everybody and welcome to the class. I'm pleased to see so many of you here today. But don't worry, there won't be any more of you! There's always a maximum of 15 in the class, and a minimum of eight. Before we start, I'd like to tell you about the course. Some of the information you'll probably know already, but some of it has changed.

Your class will still be on Tuesday evenings, but it won't start at seven o'clock, it will start at the later time of 7.30, and will end at 9.30, not nine o'clock. I hope that change is OK for everyone. Unfortunately I can't be here any earlier than that. Another change is the room. Next week we need to move to the second floor to the room opposite the art room. That's Room 26. Today is the only time we'll be here in Room 12. The coursebook will be the same as before, that is Starting French. I see some of you have already bought it – that's good. However, if you want to buy it from us, it costs £8. You can order it today, but it takes two weeks so you won't have it until 1st October.

One more thing ... during the last week of term, there is an International Evening Event at the college. There will be traditional dancing from different countries and every class is asked to provide some food. I thought we could take some French cheese, but any other suggestions are welcome.

And finally, let me remind you that most of your lessons will be completely in French. So, let's begin ...

Part 4 Preparation

07

Man So, how many followers do you have online?

Woman Um, about 10,000 at the moment.

Man Wow, that's incredible! You must be thrilled.

Woman Well, yeah, thanks. But, actually, it's not that unusual. Other people have hundreds of thousands of fans and followers! Some have millions. I mean, it feels great to have managed so much, but I can always improve.

Man Who are your typical fans?

Woman Mostly girls in their early teens, but more and more boys are following me these days.

Part 4 Practice

08

You will hear a woman called Alice Parker talking on the radio about a new shop.

Interviewer Welcome back! I'm here with Alice Parker, who is the owner of a new local business.

Alice Hello! My business is called Small World. It's in the centre of town. It's different because it isn't just a shop. At the front, we sell clothes, jewellery, wooden animals, wooden boxes, bowls and other interesting items from around the world. Then, at the back, there's a small café where we sell different kinds of tea and coffee, and home-made vegetarian snacks.

Interviewer Starting your own business is a bit of a risk, isn't it?

Audioscripts

Charles For children aged 12 and above, there's the new music club. It's on every week during the school holidays and if it's successful, the organizers are thinking of continuing it in term time. Young people bring their music to the club, exchange information about musicians and listen to and talk about music. The organizers are also planning to invite a local band to play at the club.

Interviewer Excellent! Are there any sports clubs around?

Charles Yes, of course. There's the football club, for young people who want to improve their game. There are two groups: ages 6 to 9 and 10 to 12. It's on every morning for a week – that's from 9 a.m. to 12 p.m., so children should take snacks. They'll be home in time for lunch. Drinks will be provided free of charge.

The Dance Academy is an excellent dance school that teaches ballet, jazz dance, ballroom – all kinds of dance styles, in fact. There will also be one-day courses for children aged 8+ in modern dance. The children learn new steps and routines during the course and show their parents what they've learned at the end of the day.

Keep Moving is a keep-fit club for teenagers. It's on once a week, on Mondays from 6 p.m. to 8 p.m. during term time and during the school holidays, it will be on twice a week, Mondays and Thursdays, at the same times. There will be all the usual activities including dance, team games and using the gym equipment.

Finally, FastFit Leisure Centre is having an open day on 16th August. Everything is free on this day and children of all ages can try all the facilities at the centre, including squash, tennis, basketball, diving and climbing.

Interviewer It sounds like there's a lot to do! If you have any questions ...

Practice Test 4

Listening

Part 1

1 What did the boy have to drink?

Girl Have you been to that new café on the High Street?

Boy Yes, I've been there a few times.

Girl What's the coffee like there? Is it any good?

Boy I don't know. I don't drink coffee. I usually have a milkshake or something like that when I go to a café.

Girl Oh well, are the milkshakes any good?

Boy I don't know that either, I'm afraid, because they don't sell them. The orange juice is OK. It's nothing exciting, though.

2 On which date will the author sign books?

Man We're very pleased to announce an exciting new event at our bookshop. World-famous author Karabo Drumbo is going to be here next month! She'll be reading from her latest novel, *Philo and Burke*, at 7 p.m. on April 24th. There's a separate book-signing event with Karabo on the 25th. Tickets for both can be purchased from the 21st. We recommend booking early to avoid disappointment. This is going to be very special indeed. Don't miss it!

3 Where does the woman work now?

Man Have you still got that part-time job in the cinema?

Woman I haven't worked there for a while, now. I left about a month ago and started working in the supermarket because it was better money. But it was so boring I decided to leave that as well. Then a job came up in a music shop in town so I took that. It's about the same money as I got at the cinema, but it's much more fun, and I get to listen to great tunes all day!

4 What time is the English exam?

Woman Can you all please remember that the date of your English exam has changed. It's no longer on Friday at nine o'clock. It's now on the following Monday. The time remains the same, but don't forget to get here half an hour earlier so that you can be calm and ready to begin. Don't forget French is still on Monday afternoon at one o'clock, so you're all going to have a busy day. Make sure you get plenty of rest on Saturday and Sunday.

5 What does the girl's new friend look like?

Girl Is it OK if I invite Sara to your party? She's a new girl at my gym. You've seen her. She works out on the running machines a lot.

Boy Sure, that's fine. It's always nice to meet new people. Is Sara the girl with short dark hair?

Girl She's got dark hair, but it's long and she always ties it back.

Boy Oh yeah. I know who you mean. Yes, bring her along. I look forward to meeting her.

6 Where is the man going tomorrow?

Woman I'm going shopping and then to the cinema tomorrow. Do you fancy coming? It should be a fun day.

Man I'd love to, but I've already arranged to meet some friends in town.

Woman Are you having lunch or something? I've heard that the new burger place is quite good.

Man Yeah, that's where we're meeting, actually. We all wanted to try it out. It's right next to the cinema, so maybe you could come along after the film and join us.

7 Where is the magazine?

Boy Have you finished reading the magazine I lent you?

Girl Oh yeah, thanks. It was great. Do you want it back? I've left it upstairs, in my room.

Boy Yes, please. There's an article I wanted to read in it. Can I go up to your room and get it? Is it in your bag?

Girl I took it out of there and put it on my desk. It's on top of my English book. And that reminds me. I need to do my homework. Can you bring my book down with you, please?

Part 2

8 You will hear two people talking about a painting.

Woman This is an amazing portrait, isn't it? You feel as though the woman is really looking at you.

Man I know. She has a very interesting expression on her face, too. She looks as though she's done something that she really regrets. It looks like she's very sad, but she's trying not to show it.

Woman Do you think so? I think she looks as though she's just realized the answer to a difficult problem. She looks relieved and calm to me.

Man Oh well, that's interesting. I wonder why we both have such different ideas about what she's thinking. Maybe you're a more positive person than I am!

9 You will hear a woman telling a friend about her new bag.

Woman Oh, where are my keys? I know I put them in my bag!

Man It's a very smart bag.

Woman I know. I bought it last week. It looks great, but it drives me crazy because I can never find anything in it! I thought it would be better than my old bag because it's bigger and it has so many useful pockets.

Man It certainly looks like there's a pocket for everything.

Woman There is. But I can never remember which pocket I've put things in! I hope I'll get used to it soon, or I'll have to go back to using my little old bag!

10 You will hear two friends talking about a song.

Man Not that song again! I can't get it out of my head. It seems to be playing everywhere I go at the moment. I can't seem to escape it!

Woman I know. It's really popular, isn't it? It's on every radio station, in every shop or café ... I think it's really catchy!

Man You can say that again. I keep singing it without realizing. I wish I could stop, but it's like a disease!

Woman Haha! You're funny. I'd love to hear you singing it.

Man Well, if I start, please pinch me. I really need to stop doing it!

11 You will hear two friends talking about a swimming pool.

Woman Did you enjoy your swim this morning?

Man Yes, I did, thanks. I feel really refreshed now. Have you been to the new swimming pool?

Woman Yes, I took the children there last Saturday afternoon. It was really busy, though. We could hardly find room to swim!

Man Oh, it was lovely and quiet today. You should go during the week next time – there was hardly anybody else there. The water was freezing, though! I nearly screamed when I jumped in! I had to swim really fast to warm up.

Woman Oh dear! That's certainly one way to make people get fit!

12 You will hear a woman telling a friend about her weekend.

Man Did you have a good weekend, Sarah?

Woman Yes, thank you. I visited some friends in the countryside.

Man That sounds relaxing. It's good to get out of the city sometimes, isn't it?

Woman Yes, it was very peaceful and it's wonderful to breathe clean air after all the pollution in the city. They live in a quiet village surrounded by fields and trees. Everything was so green. I found it a bit scary at night, though. When it gets dark in the countryside, it gets really dark. There are no street lights, or lights from cars and buildings.

Man I bet you had a fantastic view of the stars, though!

Woman That's true. It was really beautiful.

13 You will hear two people talking about a meal.

Man That meal was incredible. Thank you so much. You really are a wonderful cook. I ate far more than I needed to, because it was just so delicious.

Woman I'm so glad you enjoyed it. Would you like some more? There's plenty left.

Man I really couldn't. I've had two helpings already. It's very tempting to have a third, but I don't think I could possibly fit anything else in. I don't think I'll need to eat anything else for a week!

Woman Shall we go through to the living room, then?

Man Yes, that's a good idea. Don't let me get too comfortable, though. I could easily fall asleep after all that food.

Part 3

21

You will hear a radio presenter talking about a sports festival.

Man Are you wondering what to do over the summer holidays? The international sports festival starts on the 30th June, lasts for two weeks and ends on the 13th July with prize giving and fireworks. It's well worth attending. Here's why.

The fun starts on day one with a huge event in Prospect Park. Organizers will arrive early to set up, but the event for the public begins at 12 p.m. and lasts all day until six. Throughout the day, many different clubs and companies will be giving free workshops, which means you'll be able to try sports that you may never have tried before.

Some of the highlights at the opening event include skateboarding and break-dancing workshops. You might also like to bring your bike and try some extreme cycling. Before you start, an expert will check over your bike to make sure it's safe. There will also be a bike race.

To find out more information about exact times of each workshop, look on our website. You'll also be able to download a map which shows where everything will be in the park on the day.

For the remaining two weeks of the festival, you'll be able to enjoy further workshops and sessions in the area. Locations and events include water sports at River Swimming Complex, track events at the Athletics Stadium and you can also take part in indoor team games at Central Leisure. This festival is the first of its kind in our town and I really recommend you see what it's all about.

Part 4

You will hear someone talking about an organization that takes young people on expeditions.

Presenter Hello and welcome to the programme. Today, I'm talking to David Watts, who is a leader of Youth Expeditions, which is an organization that gives opportunities to young people to explore different parts of the world. David is here to try to show us that going on expeditions is a challenge that all young people can take part in, not just the super fit and super confident. David, could you tell us first about what the organization does?

David Hello. Yes, we organize expeditions to different places and invite young people aged 16–20 to go on them at as low a cost as possible. Basically we provide a grant for about 75% of the total. The aim is to develop confidence and a sense of adventure, but we also work with scientists and environmentalists. Although we want people who are keen to learn, we don't expect them to have expert scientific knowledge already.

Presenter How often do you organize expeditions?

David About three or four every year and they include month-long summer expeditions to the Arctic for those aged between 16 and 20. And then, for those over 18, there are our Arctic and desert gap-year expeditions.

Presenter Tell us about one of your most recent expeditions.

David This June, a group went to the edge of the Arctic Ocean. They went with seven leaders and a group of scientists. They cross-country skied to where they were camping and then went everywhere on foot. They took part in a series of scientific studies, investigating glaciers, rivers, plants and so on. It was a very interesting trip.

Presenter You also run competitions.

David That's right. And for this year's, three young explorers can win a place on our next expedition to the Arctic for which we'll pay the whole cost. For two months they'll live in tents and snow caves and will learn how to survive in the extreme cold. For part of the time they'll work with environmentalists on the subject of climate change, but there will also be opportunities for mountaineering and cross-country skiing. It should be a lot of fun.

Presenter So how do people enter?

David Entrants should make a short film that gives information about themselves; why they are interested in going to the Arctic, and what they hope to get out of the experience. They should send this to us by post and we'll choose a number of people to come for an interview. From those, we'll decide who has won.

Presenter It sounds like an excellent opportunity and I wish our listeners luck with that.

Practice Test 5

Listening

Part 1

1 What date does the woman's holiday begin?

Man Hi! Are you all ready for your holiday? I heard that you're going next Friday!

Woman On the 18th? No. We were planning to leave then, but my cousin's having a big party that weekend, so we're going the following Friday now.

Man Oh! That'll be the 25th, the day before I leave, too. I can't wait to get away. How long are you going for?

Woman Only ten days, but I'm really looking forward to it.

2 Where did the boy first find out about the festival?

Boy Look at this! The City Festival's on next weekend. Do you want to go?

Girl Oh yes, I really want to go, but I didn't know it was on so soon. There was an ad on TV the other day, but I didn't notice the dates.

Boy Well, I only realized it was on because my dad had last Sunday's newspaper. Here, have a look at the website and we can decide what to get tickets for.

3 What does the boy ask the girl to buy?

Girl I'm going to the shops to get some milk. Do you want me to get you anything?

Boy Yeah, can you get me some eggs, please? I'm going to make a cake for Mum's birthday.

Girl No problem. Shall I get some flour, too?

Boy Don't worry, we've got plenty in the cupboard. I was thinking of doing something different to my usual chocolate cake. Could you get a lemon and I'll try this new recipe? It looks very tasty.

4 How do you get to the bookshop?

Woman The bookshop? Oh yes, it's just off Bridge Street, next to the museum. Go straight across this roundabout and then after about 500 metres you'll have to turn right at the crossroads. Sorry, I mean left, into Bridge Street. Go down the road a little way and you'll see the museum on the corner. It's a big building with columns at the entrance. The bookshop is down a small side turning beside the museum – you can't miss it.

5 How many people live next door?

Man Hi! Where have you been?

Woman Oh, hi! I've just been chatting with our new neighbours. They seem really nice. They've got a daughter who's about Monica's age. Maybe they'll be able to play together.

Man Oh! I thought I saw an older girl there yesterday.

Woman Actually they've got three kids, but one's already left home. Anyway, the man is a teacher and his wife designs websites. So there might be a new friend for me, too!

6 Where are the new houses going to be?

Man Here's that dream house near the sea you've been waiting for. SouthEast Homes are building four luxury properties at Riversmeet. You'll be living in a quiet valley, surrounded by green fields and beautiful countryside, and the coast is just a short train ride away, so you can easily spend a day at the beach. If it's shopping or entertainment you want, you can get to the city in less than half an hour by train or bus. Check our website for more details.

7 What does the girl decide to wear to the party?

Girl Well, it's a shame you can't come to the party tonight. I'll have to go on my own. I was planning to wear those dark jeans with a black shirt. Do you think that's smart enough?

Boy How would I know? If you want to look smarter, there's that blue dress you got from the market?

Girl Brilliant idea! Much better than trousers.

Boy Well, whatever you think, but I'm sure it would be fine to just wear jeans and a T-shirt if you wanted. It's only a casual party.

Part 2

8 You will hear two friends talking about a party.

Woman Did you enjoy Kate's party last night?

Man I did, but there were loads of people there, and I hardly knew any of them. I don't know where Kate meets them all!

Woman Well, she meets a lot of people through her job, I suppose. And she's very sociable. She'll chat to anyone, so she makes new friends everywhere she goes.

Man I know! Not like me. I'm too shy to just go up and talk to new people. That's why I spent most of the night talking to you!

Woman Oh, thanks! I thought it was because I'm great company!

9 You will hear a man telling a friend about his holiday plans.

Man I can't wait to escape from the city and go on holiday next week. It's going to be fantastic!

Woman Where are you going?

Man I'm going to a quiet little village in Italy, high up in the mountains. I can't stand lying on a beach on holiday and staying in resorts full of tourists. I want to experience what life is like for the locals in the places I visit – to eat what they eat and do what they do. That's how you really get to know a place.

Woman It sounds lovely. I hope you have a great time!

10 You will hear two people talking about a recipe.

Boy Oh, it's no good. I just can't get it right.

Girl What's the matter?

Boy I'm trying to make the cookies my grandma used to bake for me when I was little. My mum gave me the recipe. I've followed all the instructions, but I just can't make them taste the same. I wonder if the measurements in the recipe are wrong. Or maybe I'm using different brands of ingredients, and that's making the cookies taste different.

Girl Perhaps your grandma had a secret ingredient which she didn't tell your mum about.

Boy Do you know, I bet you're right! That's just like my grandma! I wonder what it could be ...

11 You will hear two people talking about a gym.

Woman What do you think of the new gym in town?

Man It's great! I've been there a few times now. The equipment is very modern, and everything is very clean and smart.

Woman It certainly seems very popular. It's always full of people.

Man Yes, it does get very busy, but you never have to wait for equipment. There are enough machines for everyone.

Woman That's true. I just wish there were a few more lockers in the changing rooms. By the time I get there, they're all taken, so there's nowhere for me to leave my things. I suppose I'll have to start going earlier.

12 You will hear a woman telling a friend about her new hobby.

Man How are you getting on with your sewing?

Woman I'm actually getting really good at it! I've made a few things, now. I made a skirt for my mum, and a pair of curtains for my friend's new flat. I even made this bag. What do you think?

Man That's amazing! It must save you a fortune now that you can make your own clothes.

Woman Well, that's what I was hoping, but it's often just as expensive to buy the material and the other bits and pieces. Sometimes it's cheaper to buy something ready-made in the shops. But the great thing about making your own clothes is that nobody else has the same items as you.

Man That's true. Your clothes will be one of a kind.

13 You will hear two friends talking about a TV show.

Man Oh, why do they do that at the end of every series? I hate it when they end the show just as something terrible or exciting is about to happen. They leave you desperate to know what happens next, and you have to wait months for the next series to start so that you can find out!

Woman That's the whole idea, isn't it? They don't want you to forget to watch the new series.

Man Well, there's no chance of that! I'm going to be wondering about the next episode all summer now.

Woman I'm sure you'll find something to take your mind off it before the next series starts!

Part 3

25

You will hear a recorded message giving information about a museum.

Woman This is the information line for the Dorset Chocolate Museum: the home of chocolate lovers and the ideal place to spend an afternoon.

Do you know who used cocoa beans as money in the 16th century, or where chocolate was drunk as a medicine? At the Dorset Chocolate Museum, you'll find out about all this and more. Our fascinating displays will guide you through the history of chocolate making from its earliest use in South America to the modern day.

Then move on to the demonstration area of our small family-run factory. Here you can watch our skilled chocolate-makers making a variety of chocolate bars, as well as other sweets, and you can even have a try at making your own.

We open seven days a week from 12 midday till 6 p.m., except in July and August when we are open until 8 p.m. From September to December we are open at weekends only. We are closed throughout January, but open again from the first of February.

Admission is £10 for adults and £5 for children up to the age of 16, while children under five are free. Students pay £2 less, so that's £8, but only if they have a student ID card.

Special reduced entrance fees are available for groups of ten or more people. We can also make special arrangements for schools on weekdays between 12 and 4 p.m. All groups will be provided with a private tour guide, and at the end each member of the group will receive a bag of lovely hand-made chocolates.

Our special range of chocolate boxes and bars is always available to buy in our gift shop. For more details phone the gift shop on 01632 960054.

Audioscripts

Part 4

You will hear a chef talking about his career.

Interviewer What does it take to be a head chef? Paul Heaton is here to tell us all about it.

Paul Thanks! I didn't enjoy school that much, and I decided quite early on that I was going to leave as soon as I could, which was at 16. I tried a few other things, including the local supermarket, but nothing really interested me until I got a job as a kitchen assistant. I was a fresh-faced 17-year-old when I turned up at the Grand Hotel. It was hard, dirty work and the pay wasn't great either. On the positive side, I was in a really busy kitchen where the top chefs were highly skilled and during my breaks I could watch and learn. I was fascinated by all the equipment and the unlikely stories of people injuring themselves with kitchen tools.

Interviewer I imagine that kitchen assistants don't work from nine to five.

Paul No! I had to get used to long hours and working late. They needed me when the kitchen got busy, around twelve o'clock, which doesn't sound bad, but I sometimes wouldn't finish until two o'clock the next morning. I'd spend most of the time cleaning the kitchen equipment or preparing food for the chefs to use. I must've washed and prepared literally millions of carrots and potatoes.

Interviewer But those days are behind you now, aren't they?

Paul Yes, these days I'm a head chef, so I'm responsible for organizing the kitchen. This includes preparing the menus, selecting and training staff and keeping the kitchen in good working order. And, I still love to cook of course. But now I don't have to do it every day, but can choose to do it when I really want to.

Interviewer What advice would you give to anyone thinking of becoming a chef?

Paul You have to be able to work in a team, whether you're cleaning the floor or grilling a steak. You must be prepared to deal with stressful situations. And you have to be able to think quickly – if the fish you wanted to use for your main dish doesn't arrive, you've got to invent something completely different.

People sometimes think that preparing food in a first-class restaurant is a complicated and difficult thing to do. This is partly true – there's a lot to think about and your work needs to be right every time – but the key to success is to buy the best and the freshest food available and keep things simple.

Practice Test 6

Listening

Part 1

27

1 What is the woman going to buy today?

Woman I'm going shopping in town this afternoon. I need to get a present for Jan. It's her birthday next week.

Man Oh, really? What are you thinking of getting her?

Woman I've already got her a bag and I thought about buying her a book or a scarf, too. What do you think?

Man I don't think she reads much, so I think a scarf would probably be better.

Woman OK. Thanks. I'll see if I can find something she'll like.

2 What time did Sarah finish work today?

Man You're home late, Sarah! I was starting to get worried about you. It's nine o'clock!

Woman Yes, I know, I didn't catch a train until 8.00.

Man Were you working all that time? That's a long day for you!

Woman No, I left work at 6.00, as usual, but I met Tess on my way to the station. We got chatting and decided to go for a pizza. I hadn't seen her for ages, so we had a lot to talk about.

3 What is the woman planning to do at the weekend?

Man Are you meeting Jess and Pete on Saturday?

Woman Yes, but we aren't going to the restaurant now.

Man Oh, why not? I've heard the food there is great.

Woman Yes, I've heard that, too, but we've decided to have a picnic in the park instead. I was going to cook a meal for them but I think the weather's going to be good this weekend, so we thought it would be nice to eat outside.

4 What is the weather going to be like this afternoon?

Woman After a bright and sunny morning, clouds are beginning to form and it looks like we're going to see some rain later today, probably from around two o'clock, so don't forget your umbrellas. The rain will be light, however, and no thunderstorms are expected. It will clear up in the evening, and there'll be light cloud for the rest of the night, with a clear day tomorrow.

5 How did the man find out about the play?

Woman That was a fantastic play. Thank you for recommending it.

Man You're very welcome. I'm glad you enjoyed it.

Woman How did you hear about it? Did you read a review about it?

Man No, I know there have been some good reviews in the newspapers, but I didn't see them. My friend John heard about it on the radio and emailed me and suggested I went to see it. He'll be pleased to hear that we both enjoyed it.

6 When is the man's first guitar lesson?

Woman Have you started guitar lessons yet?

Man Not yet. They've been delayed. They were going to start on the 15th, but the teacher was ill.

Woman Oh dear. I hope she's better now.

Man Yes, she is, and she's going to give two lessons in one week this week to catch up. The first one will be on the 21st and the second will be on the 23rd.

Woman Great! I look forward to hearing you play something soon.

Man Haha! It might be a while before I can play a song!

7 How does the woman usually keep fit?

Man Hi, Sally. It's great seeing you here. I didn't know you liked running!

Woman I don't! I go to the gym most days, but it's closed at the moment. They're doing some building work. I've got to do something while it's closed and I haven't got a bike, so I thought I'd better try running.

Man Oh well, why don't you join me? I'm here every morning, and it'll be good to have some company.

Part 2

28

8 You will hear two people talking about the weather.

Woman Oh dear. It's raining again. I'm getting really fed up with all this wet weather. I wanted to go for a picnic this weekend.

Man Well, the weather forecast says that the rain is going to stop by Saturday morning, and we're going to have a few sunny days.

Woman Really? I'll believe that when I see it. I don't trust the weather forecast.

Man I don't know. They're pretty accurate these days. I rely on the weather app on my phone to tell me when I need to take an umbrella with me!

Woman Well, I hope that you and your weather app are right. A few sunny days would be lovely.

Audioscripts

9 You will hear a woman telling a friend about her dreams.

Man Where do you see yourself in five years' time?

Woman Oh, I'd love to be living in a little house in the countryside, painting every day and making a living from selling my art. It's a shame there's not much money in painting.

Man I'm sure you could make money. Your work is very good.

Woman Thank you. But you can't guarantee that you'll make enough to live on when you're an artist. It's a big risk to take. I think I'd need to have a lot of money in the bank before I took the chance and bought my little cottage, so I expect I'll be working in the city for a few more years!

10 You will hear two friends talking about a trip.

Man I know we were planning to drive to the airport and leave our car there while we were on holiday, but have you seen how much airport parking costs?

Woman I know it's expensive. But what else can we do?

Man We could take the train to the airport.

Woman We could do, but we'd have to change trains twice, with all our luggage. And if there's a delay, we could miss our flight.

Man Good point. I know! Why don't we ask someone to give us a lift? We've taken David to the airport loads of times!

Woman That's true! Let's ask David if he'll drive us there and pick us up next week.

11 You will hear a man telling a friend about his job.

Woman I think you're very brave to work as a firefighter. You must face danger every day.

Man No, not every day. Most of the calls we get are not actually for fires. We rescue people from all sorts of situations. When we do get called to a fire, we have all the right equipment. The biggest danger is that a firefighter isn't fit enough. It's really important to keep fit in this job.

Woman Yes, it must be. And I expect communication is important, too.

Man Oh yes. You need to communicate with your team and trust each other, too. If you work together well, then you are a lot safer.

12 You will hear two people talking about a supermarket.

Man How often do you shop here at RightPrice?

Woman I usually come here once a week to do a big shop. It's got all the things I need for the family – food, cleaning products, even clothes.

Man Can you always find everything you want here?

Woman Almost always. I mean, the range of products is excellent, and the supermarket usually has all the things on my shopping list. The only thing is that they keep moving things around. Just when I get used to where everything is, they change things around and put all the products in different places. That can make a shopping trip last longer than it should, which annoys me.

13 You will hear two friends talking about a computer game.

Boy Look at this new game! Isn't it fantastic! The characters look like real people.

Girl Wow! It's just like watching a film! That's fantastic. Is it good fun to play?

Boy It's great! The puzzles are a bit difficult, though. Sometimes it can take me days to work out what I need to do to get to the next stage of the game.

Girl Well, you don't want it to be too easy, or you'll finish the game too fast!

Boy That's true, but I like to find out what happens next in the story. I get bored if I have to wait too long to move on in the game.

Part 3

29

You will hear a woman talking to a group of tourists about their holiday.

Woman Good afternoon. It's lovely to see you all. You've certainly got some great weather for your holiday! Now, in a moment you'll be shown up to your rooms. Then in about an hour's time, at about one o'clock, a light lunch will be served in the dining room. The dining room is at the front of the hotel, next to the bar. For your information, breakfast is served between 7 a.m. and 9 a.m., lunch is from 12 p.m. to 3 p.m. and dinner is served in the evening between 8 p.m. and 11 p.m. Traditional music is played by local musicians twice a week during dinner.

Now a few words about activities. There are trips most mornings which you can join, if you like. These include visits to local places of interest, including the ruins and various monuments. I'll give you more details about those later. You can also visit an outdoor market where you'll be able to find souvenirs to take home. That's only on once a week on Thursday, so don't miss it. In the afternoons, you can either walk to the beach, which is just five minutes away, or you can relax by the hotel swimming pool.

That's it for now, I think. I hope you like your rooms. Please stay behind if you have any questions. Otherwise, I'll see you in the dining room in about an hour. Thank you very much.

Part 4

You will hear an interview with the manager of a new leisure centre.

Interviewer Welcome to the Leisure Programme. Today I'm interviewing Jack Hutchinson, the manager of a new leisure centre that opened last month. Welcome to the programme, Jack.

Jack Thank you.

Interviewer Jack, there are several leisure centres in this area. Why do you think yours has become so popular already? Is it because it has such a fantastic gym?

Jack No, I don't think it's because of the gym, although the gym is excellent. I think it's because so many articles have been written about us in the local newspapers. People want to see if we're as good as the journalists say.

Interviewer So, tell us about the centre.

Jack Well, let's start with the pools – we've already got a very good, large swimming pool with a diving area. There's also a smaller training pool, which is for children and for adults having lessons, and there are plans to build a fun pool with slides for children.

Interviewer And what about this amazing gym?

Jack The equipment is excellent and we have experienced staff who are very happy to give advice.

Interviewer Are the staff there all the time?

Jack They're usually there for two hours in the afternoon and an hour in the evening. We're hoping to increase the time they're available when we employ more staff.

Interviewer What about courts?

Jack There are indoor courts for tennis, badminton, volleyball and basketball. The outdoor tennis courts aren't quite ready, but they'll be available next week.

Interviewer What about classes?

Jack There are swimming classes at all levels, karate, aerobics and keep-fit. We also offer one-day scuba-diving courses at the pool. They're given by instructors from the local diving school. I've done one myself and so have most of our swimming instructors. I can highly recommend them.

Interviewer So, in what way do you think your leisure centre is better than others?

Jack The facilities are of a very high quality. We offer a wide range of different activities and we have a café that sells good, healthy food.

Interviewer Well, ... other centres offer all that, too.

Jack Yes, but they don't offer our prices. Like other centres, we offer discounts to students and the over 60s, but people can also buy a membership card for just £15 a month. For this, you can use all the facilities as often as you like. You pay much more for membership in other centres.

Interviewer That sounds very good. Thank you for coming in, Jack ...

Answer key

Answer key

for Preparation

PREPARATION ANSWER KEY

Reading

Part 1 p8

1 **A** 4 **B** 5 **C** 2 **D** 1 **E** 3
2 **A** 5 **B** 2 **C** 1 **D** 3 **E** 4
3 **1** unbelievable **2** as well; in addition **3** fix **4** daily **5** certain; sure **6** underneath **7** attempt **8** discuss **9** beside **10** not permitted; allowed
4 **1** C **2** A **3** C

Part 2 p12

1 **1** five **2** eight **3** three **4** cross them out **5** mark them
2 **Nouns:** ability / emergency / salary
Verbs: affect / collect / provide
Adverbs: already / lately / particularly
Adjectives: guilty / interested / marvellous
3 **1** Bernie wants to find a small hotel that is not too expensive.
2 There is room for 25 students in the class. The course starts on 2nd May and is suitable for 15- and 16-year-olds.
3 Pedro wants to have the party by the swimming pool, but several family members prefer the beach.
4 Marcus is studying at home because he he's had a broken leg since last month's football match.
5 Kei and Joe are meeting on Thursday. Joe wants to meet at noon, but Kei isn't free until half past twelve. They might meet on Friday instead.
4.1 **1** yes **2** yes **3** yes **4** no **5** no
4.2 **1** yes **2** yes **3** yes **4** no **5** no

Part 3 p16

1 **1** B **2** A **3** C **4** B **5** C
2A **1** specific information **2** fast **3** don't read **4** probably won't
2B **1** skim **2** don't read **3** don't pay **4** specific details
3 **1** C **2** A **3** B **4** D
4 **A** 4 **B** 2 **C** 3 **D** 1

Part 4 p20

1 **1** C **2** A **3** C **4** B **5** A **6** B
2 **A** 4 **B** 5 **C** 3 **D** 6 **E** 2 **F** 1
3 **1** On the other **2** For example **3** Significantly **4** Secondly **5** The reason **6** Furthermore

Part 5 p23

1 **1** C **2** B **3** B **4** A **5** D **6** A
2 **1** D **2** C **3** A **4** B
3 **1** D **2** F **3** A **4** E **5** C **6** B
4 **1** C **2** D **3** A

Part 6 p26

1 **1** A **2** B **3** C **4** A **5** C **6** B
2 **1** like OR want **2** who **3** or **4** at **5** mind **6** what
3 **1** This is urgent. Please call me back so soon as you can.
2 The event sounded like fun, so we decided to make part in it.
3 Who do you prefer, pizza or pasta?
4 The season I like the more is summer.
5 You have to pay for the hotel room on advance.
6 It rained all day and I didn't feel for doing anything.
4 **1** This is urgent. Please call me back **as** soon as you can.
2 The event sounded like fun, so we decided to **take** part in it.
3 **Which** do you prefer, pizza or pasta?
4 The season I like the **most** is summer.
5 You have to pay for the hotel room **in** advance.
6 It rained all day and I didn't feel **like** doing anything.
5 **1** few **2** of **3** little **4** At **5** if **6** more **7** some **8** takes

Writing

Part 1 p29

2 **1** E **2** B **3** C **4** A **5** D
3 **A** 3 **B** 8 **C** 4 **D** 7 **E** 6 **F** 1 **G** 5 **H** 2

Part 2a p32

1 **1** start **2** opinion **3** reason **4** mention **5** enough **6** most **7** paragraph **8** end
2 Students' own answers.
3 **1** B **2** A **3** B **4** both **5** neither **6** B **7** A **8** A **9** B **10** A
4 **1** Without a doubt **2** I know this because **3** Personally, **4** The reason is that

Part 2b p34

1 **A** 5 **B** 2 **C** 6 **D** 3 **E** 1 **F** 4
2 **A** 2 **B** 3 **C** 1
3 **Past continuous:** was studying / were crashing / was coming
Past Perfect: had been / had gone / had finished
Past Simple: was (in) / began / were (open) / didn't join / was (loud) / rushed / closed / ended / was (calm) / heard / screamed
4 **1** incredibly **2** brand **3** specially **4** excitedly **5** completely **6** slowly **7** miserable

Listening

Part 1 p37

1 **1** **1** C **2** A **3** B
2 **1** A **2** C **3** B
3 **1** C **2** B **3** A
4 **1** A **2** C **3** B
5 **1** B **2** C **3** A
2 **1** C **2** A **3** B **4** C
3 **1** like the most **2** final **3** didn't end until **4** at the moment

Part 2 p41

1 **1** You will hear two friends talking about a new shopping mall. What does the man think of it?
2 You will hear two friends talking about a film they watched. What did the girl like best about it?
3 You will hear a boy telling his aunt about a book he's read. How does he feel about it?

Answer key

4 You will hear two friends talking about a website. What do they agree on?
5 You will hear a man telling a friend about a problem. What does the woman advise him to do?

2 **1, 4, 5, 7**

3 **1** D **2** E **3** A **4** C **5** B

4 **1** **A** doesn't think **B** thinks **C** doesn't think **D** thinks
2 **A** doesn't agree **B** doesn't agree **C** doesn't agree **D** agrees
3 **A** likes **B** liked **C** didn't like **D** didn't like

Part 3 p45

1 **1** B **2** C **3** C **4** B **5** C

2 **1** B **2** B **3** B **4** A **5** C

3 **1** The event took place on the ~~13rd~~ of May. *13th*
2 There was a statue ~~nex~~ to the fountain. *next*
3 Participants were given ~~halve~~ an hour for lunch. *half*
4 They can only accept ~~too~~ more students on this course. *two*
5 The accident happened last ~~Novembur~~. *November*
6 They met in the new café across from the ~~statiom~~. *station*
7 The organizers had to decide which ~~celebritys~~ to invite. *celebrities*
8 She didn't want to ~~loose~~ it, so she kept it in a safe place. *lose*

Part 4 p48

1 **1** overall gist
2 someone's attitude
3 specific information
4 specific information
5 detailed meaning
6 someone's opinion

2 **1** D **2** F **3** A **4** E **5** C **6** B

3 **1** **A** 10,000 people follow her online.
B There's nothing special about 10,000.
~~**C** She feels good about what she has achieved.~~
D Others have hundreds of thousands!
~~**E** She wants to do better.~~
F Some people have millions.
G Teenage girls typically follow her.
2 ~~**A** She has 10,000 online followers.~~
B It's fairly common to have 10,000 followers.
C She is proud of her achievement.
D She's happy, but she wants to do more.
~~**E** There are people with millions of followers.~~
~~**F** A lot of teenage girls follow her.~~
~~**G** Some boys have started to follow her too.~~

Speaking

Part 1 p51

1 **1** name **2** What **3** spell **4** Where **5** with **6** Do

2 **1** My name is Chris.
2 My surname is Potter.
3 It's spelt P.O.T.T.E.R. / You spell it P.O.T.T.E.R.
4 I come from Canada.
5 I live with my mother and brother.
6 Yes, I do. / No, I don't.

3 **1** B **2** A **3** B **4** C **5** B **6** A

4 Students' own answers.

5 **A** 3 **B** 1 **C** 4 **D** 2

Part 2 p53

1 **1** at **2** on **3** in **4** in **5** at **6** in **7** on **8** in

2 **1** A, C **2** A, B **3** A, C **4** B, C **5** A, B **6** A, C

3 **1** E **2** C **3** D **4** F **5** A **6** B

4 **1** is **2** looks **3** are **4** are having / 're having **5** is standing **6** has

5 **1** foreground **2** number 23 jersey **3** getting up **4** number 7 **5** in the air **6** concentrating hard **7** long-sleeved top **8** holding onto it **9** on the ground **10** helmet **11** reaching down **12** background

Part 3 p56

1 **A** 4 **B** 1 **C** 5 **D** 2 **E** 6 **F** 3

2 **Agreeing:** I think you're right. / It's a great idea. / That's true because ... / Yes, I agree with that.
Disagreeing: I don't think that would work. / I'm afraid I don't agree. / Sorry I don't see it that way. / Well, I disagree because ...
Making suggestions: How about ... / Maybe we could ... / What if we ... / Why don't we ...

3 2, 3, 6

4 Students' own answers.

5, 6 **1** Personally; What do you think?
2 Maybe; How does that sound to you?
3 I see what you mean.; feel
4 Do you agree?
5 what do you think we should do?
6 concerned

Part 4 p58

1 **1** C **2** B **3** A **4** A

2 **1** Do you think that events for charity are important? (Why?)
2 Have you ever taken part in a charity event?
3 Which do you think is better: making the government or the public responsible for charity?
4 Do you enjoy supporting charity events? (Why)

3 **1** C **2** E **3** F **4** A **5** D **6** B

4 **1** experience **2** explain **3** mean **4** don't agree **5** far **6** go along **7** point

5 **1** If you ask **nicely**, everyone will help.
2 It's **always** difficult at the beginning.
3 They **really** shouldn't drive so fast.
4 It seems to be an **extremely** expensive operation.
5 It's a product I would **definitely** buy for my parents

6 **1** B **2** A **3** B

Speaking Paper: Model Answers

Part 1 Phase 1

1 What's your name?
My name is Chris.

2 What is your surname?
My surname is Potter.

3 How do you spell that?
It's spelt P.O.T.T.E.R.

4 Where do you come from?
I come from Canada.

5 Who do you live with?
I live with my mother and my brother.

6 Do you study?
Yes, I do.

Part 1 Phase 2

1 **What do you like doing with your friends?**
Well, it depends on the time of year. In the summer, we do stuff outside, like cycling and having barbeques. In the winter, we watch a lot of TV.

2 **Tell us about a celebrity you like.**
I don't really care about film stars, but I'm a big sports fan. I love Kei Nishikori. He's a tennis player from Japan. He's been playing since he was five years old!

3 **How often do you use your mobile phone?**
Um, I don't make many calls, but I text quite a lot, and I check social media pretty often. I suppose it's a few hours every day, altogether.

4 **Which do you like better, Saturday or Sunday?**
I'm always busy doing a lot of things on Saturdays. But on Sundays I can really relax so that's the day I prefer. I stay in my pyjamas and eat snacks all day.

Part 2

Tell us what you can see in your photograph.

Candidate 1 This photograph shows a scene from a football match. It looks like an exciting game! In the foreground, I can see two players. The nearest one is wearing the number 23 jersey, which is dark blue. He's also wearing white shorts and long blue socks. He's on the ground, but it looks like he's getting up. The other person I can see is the number 7 player. He's wearing a white jersey with red shorts and long white socks. He's actually in the air, and so is the ball! I think he's about to kick it. I can see that he's really concentrating hard. The football stadium is in the background. It's completely full of fans! I know it's night-time because the stadium lights are on.

Candidate 2 In this picture, I can see that there's been a road accident. There is a woman lying on the road. She's wearing a long-sleeved top, and her right leg is injured or sore because she's holding on to it. Luckily, it doesn't seem to be too serious because she's sitting up. Her bicycle is lying on the ground behind her. In the bottom right corner of the photo there is a white bicycle helmet. In the middle of the picture there's a man wearing a blue jumper. He's reaching down to help the woman, and he's also talking on his mobile phone. Right behind him there's a dark-coloured car with one door open. In the backgound, there are some buildings.

Part 3

Some local families in the town have lost their homes in a fire. You and your partner want to hold a charity event to help the families, but you don't have much time to organize it. Here are some possibilities. Talk together about these ideas. Decide which would be the best to do and the quickest to arrange.

Eva OK, so we need to organize a charity event. Personally, I like the idea of a sports day. Most people enjoy sports, and it would be fun. What do you think?

Tom Um, I agree that it would be nice, but I'm afraid I don't think it's very practical. I mean, I don't think we'd have enough time to set it all up, would we? Maybe we could arrange a charity car wash instead. How does that sound to you?

Eva Well, first of all, I think you're right about the sports day. And, secondly, yeah, it's true that people like to have their cars washed, but ...

Tom But you don't think it's a good idea?

Eva Well, look, the main reason is the time of year, you know? Because, these days, the weather is awful. It's pretty cold and it rains a lot; I can't imagine standing outside washing cars all day.

Tom Yeah, I see what you mean. You're right. How do you feel about the idea of a cake sale, then? That's something we could do indoors.

Eva Yes, you're right about that. And we could bake a lot of stuff ourselves, couldn't we?

Tom Definitely! I'd say we could ask local bakeries and supermarkets give us some cakes, too. I'm sure they'd help.

Eva True, there's just one thing, though.

Tom Oh? What's that?

Eva I'm just not sure we'd make much money selling cakes. Do you agree?

Tom Yeah, I do. Good point. What do you think we should do?

Eva As far as I'm concerned, a quiz is the best option. For one thing, it would be quick to organize, like, we could get the questions off the Internet.

Tom That's right. And, for another, it'd be easy enough to find a venue.

Eva Great. So you don't mind not having an art exhibition?

Tom No, as far as I'm concerned, we should definitely do a quiz. I wasn't in favour of the meet-a-celebrity idea, either.

Eva Agreed. I don't know any celebrities!

Part 4

1 **Do you think that events for charity are important? (Why?)**
In my opinion they are very important. The reason is that there are people in the world who are suffering, and, without charity events, they would suffer even more.

2 **Have you ever taken part in a charity event?**
Yes, I took part in one last year. A local charity needed a new van, and a group of us wanted to help. We played table tennis for 24 hours! It was tiring, but fun. People gave us quite a bit of money so it was worth the effort.

3 **Which do you think is better: making the government or the public responsible for charity?**
As far as I'm concerned, it should be both. Governments definitely have a responsibility, but it shouldn't stop with politicians because society is better when members of the public help each other.

4 **Do you enjoy supporting charity events? (Why?)**
Yes, I do. The reason is that I like helping people who are suffering.

Answer key

Answer key

for Practice Tests 1–6

PRACTICE TEST ANSWER KEY

Practice Test 1

Reading

Part 1 p10

1 B **Correct. *Repairs* will delay cyclists for *24 hours.***
A There will be delays for *24 hours*, not for the whole week.
C The notice doesn't say that the lane is closed.

2 C **Correct. Suzie asks Harry if he wants to *borrow* [her] *notes.***
A Suzie said it was a *good lecture*, and she wasn't ill.
B Harry *missed* the lecture because he was ill.

3 A **Correct. Students need to *complete an application form by Thursday.***
B The notice doesn't say when the lessons *start*.
C *Thursday* refers to the day when the applications need to be in.

4 B **Correct. If you spend *over £15*, you can get a *free bottle of cola or lemonade.***
A Only customers who spend more than £15 receive the free offer.
C The offer is with *takeaway* orders, not with orders to eat in the restaurant.

5 A **Correct. The restaurant has employed *new Italian chefs* recently.**
B There is no information about the restaurant moving.
C The owner hasn't opened a restaurant in Italy.

Part 2 p14

6 **E Sasha / Checkmate!**
want food, music and dancing: *three-course meal followed by a disco*
20 people from work: *group bookings welcome*
can't spend too much: *special offer: pay for eight tickets and get two free*

7 **H Carlos / Chez Jean-Paul**
going out with his girlfriend: *perfect for a quiet night out for couples*
wants international food: *delicious French food*
doesn't want a live band: *carefully selected playlist*
doesn't cost too much: *low prices*

8 **A Henry and Clara / The Carriage Hotel**
somewhere expensive and special: *is perfect for a special night out, prices are high*
would like to stay overnight: *there is a small discount for guests of the hotel*
their daughter doesn't eat meat: *they offer a good selection of vegetarian options*

9 **F Tanya and Sam / Friday Feasts**
want to feel comfortable with their children: *relax in a family restaurant*
early evening, not too expensive: *cheap prices, children eat free between six and seven*

10 **D Ayesha and Jane / Let's Go**
somewhere lively: *popular with young people*
can eat cheaply: *the food isn't expensive*
listen to modern music: *pop music is played every night*
going out afterwards: *closes at ten*

Part 3 p18

11 B **Correct. She was *always telling jokes* in class.**
A She was funny, not her friends.
C She annoyed the teachers, but she doesn't say that she disliked them.
D Her jokes were good because she made people laugh.

12 C **Correct. She worked in a fast food restaurant and took acting classes in the evenings.**
A She worked in a restaurant.
B She took acting classes.
D She performed in theatres.

13 D **Correct. She's worked in comedy clubs, theatres and on TV.**
A Sometimes the audience didn't laugh at her jokes.
B Doing theatre work is harder than being on TV.
C Her first job after leaving school was in a fast food restaurant.

14 B **Correct. It helps her to think, and when she returns, her head is full of ideas.**
A *Walking is a great way to relax*, but she doesn't say it makes her laugh.
C She says that comedy, not walking, takes away worries.
D When she has no ideas, she goes walking to fill her mind with ideas.

15 C **Correct. She's had a successful career and is always looking for new ideas.**
A She doesn't say that she's always laughing.
B She has time to relax and has an active life apart from her work.
D She enjoys theatre work more than TV.

Part 4 p22

16 D 17 F 18 A 19 C 20 E

Part 5 p25

21 **which**
***Special designs* are objects and take the relative pronoun *which*.**
When, *who* and *whose* are relative pronouns, but don't refer to objects.

22 **invited**
***Invited to* means that people can choose whether to attend or not, and the event is not compulsory.**
Called and *demanded* are used in situations where something is necessary or compulsory; *requested* simply means *asked*.

23 **Many**
***Many* is required to agree with the plural noun *designs*.**
Lot needs an indefinite article: *a lot of*. *Much* is used with uncountable nouns. *Each* is used before a singular noun.

24 **provide**
***Provide* completes the verb phrase *provide someone with something*.**
Produce, *design* and *give* don't form a verb phrase with the preposition *with* in this context.

25 **Although**
***Although* completes the subordinate clause of contrast.**
Even needs *though* in this context (*even though*). *So* and *But* are used to link two main clauses, but cannot be used with a subordinate clause.

Answer key

26 ended

The event ended means that it *finished*.

Left, *done* and *completed* would need to be passive in order to follow the subject *event*.

Part 6 p28

27 for
28 If
29 so
30 more
31 most
32 with

Writing

Part 1 p31

Below is a model answer for Question 1 and some comments on it.

Model answer

Hi Tom,

I'm looking forward to going camping with you, too.

I think staying in a tent is a great idea. It will be much better than staying in a cabin. I have a big tent. We can both sleep in it.

I'm not very good at swimming, so I'm afraid I can't go sailing on the lake with you. I'm having swimming lessons, but I'm still learning at the moment! But we can go walking in the forest instead.

Please can you tell me what I need to bring for the camping trip?

Write again soon!

Marcos

(100 words)

Comments

Marcos has answered all parts of the question, and his answer is of the correct length. He has used appropriate opening and closing remarks in his email, and his response is well organized and easy to understand. Marcos uses different structures and appropriate vocabulary in his email and he has not made any grammatical or spelling errors.

Part 2 p36

Below is a model answer for Question 2 and some comments on it.

Model answer

I read books in the evening or on the beach in summer. I love reading funny books. I like books with funny stories and funny characters in them because they make me laugh. I don't like scary books with horror stories or ghosts.

I don't like reading e-books. I prefer reading paper books. I don't want to read on a screen. I like to hold a book and turn the pages. It's also nice to look at the cover and see the picture on the front. I usually get books from the library or buy books from my local bookshop.

(100 words)

Comments

This is a very good attempt. The writer answers the question. Her response is well organized and easy to understand. She uses a good range of structures (*I love reading .... because ...*, *I don't like ...*, etc.) and vocabulary (*characters*, *e-books*, *pages*, *cover*, *screen*, *library*, *bookshop*). There are no grammatical or spelling errors, and the article is of the correct length.

Below is a model answer for Question 3 and some comments on it.

Model answer

There was no one at the party when I arrived. It was a bit strange. There was food on the table and there were a lot of balloons and presents. But where were all the guests? Then I looked at my invitation. The party was today, but it didn't start until five o'clock. I realized that I was one hour early! I left the party and went to a café. I had a coffee and a sandwich, and I relaxed for an hour. When I returned to the party, there were a lot of people dancing and laughing. We all had a wonderful time!

(102 words)

Comments

This is a good story of the correct length, which answers the question and uses the first sentence correctly. The writer uses different structures (*There was food ...*, *The party was today but ...*, *So, ... and ...*, etc.). There is a variety of appropriate vocabulary (*invitation*, *balloons*, *presents*, *guests*, etc.), and no grammatical or spelling errors. The story is well structured and easy to understand.

Listening

Part 1 p39

1 **C Correct. The man explains that the wedding is *on the 17th*, but he will be travelling before that.**
A Mike's party is *on the 14th*.
B The man is travelling to see his brother *on the 15th*.

2 **A Correct. They have enough milk and bread, so the woman only needs to buy butter.**
B They have a lot of bread, and the man asks her not to buy any more.
C They have enough milk because the woman bought some the day before.

3 **B Correct. The man changes his shopping plan and agrees to go to the cinema on Saturday.**
A The man decides to go shopping in the evening rather than on Saturday as he originally planned.
C The birthday party is on Sunday.

4 **B Correct. The woman says she sat in her garden on Sunday.**
A The man, not the woman, says that he *went to the beach*.
C The woman went for a picnic on *Saturday*.

5 **A Correct. The man booked his holiday with a travel agent by phone.**
B He doesn't like using the Internet for *booking things*.
C He booked by phone; he's going to the travel agency to pick up the tickets.

6 **B Correct. The exam *starts at two o'clock*.**
A It's one o'clock *now*.
C The man thinks the exam starts at four o'clock, but it *finishes* then.

7 **A Correct. The police decided to *close a section of the road*.**
B The rain *did not have much effect* on the traffic.
C The traffic is *still fairly light*, and people have not started *returning home from work* yet.

Part 2 p43

8 **C Correct. They say that they *prefer her earlier songs.***
A They *prefer her earlier songs.*
B The man says that Kaylee has *a great voice.*

9 **B Correct. They say that the chairs are *uncomfortable* and *hard.***
A They say that some of the dishes *have funny names*, but the staff explained what they all were.
C They say that the staff are *cheerful and polite.*

10 **C Correct. She says that she finds the hours *a bit much*, and she struggles *to stay awake until home time.***
A She says that the boss *isn't too bad.*
B She says that the work is *interesting.*

11 **A Correct. The girl says that she wishes he *wouldn't give* [them] *so much homework on a Friday.***
B She says that he *explains things really well.*
C She says that he *makes the lessons interesting.*

12 **B Correct. He says that he *was expecting there to be a bit more action.***
A He says that the trailer they saw last week *made the film look more exciting.*
C He says that the film *was funny.*

13 **A Correct. She says that they *always improve* the website.**
B The boy says that every time he gets used to using the website, it changes.
C The girl says that the website has some *cool new features.*

Part 3 p47

14 15 / fifteen
15 9.30
16 art room
17 Starting
18 October
19 food

Part 4 p50

20 **B Correct. Alice's business is a shop with *a small café* at the back.**
A The business is a shop and a café, not a restaurant.
C The business sells *items from around the world*, but it isn't a travel agency.

21 **C Correct. Alice wanted to be independent and *work for* [herself].**
A She says that you *can't be sure that you'll make any money.*
B She already has *good experience of the business world.*

22 **A Correct. She got the idea when she was travelling in Kenya.**
B She was at a street market in Kenya, not England.
C She has travelled in India, but she hasn't lived there.

23 **B Correct. She looks for things that are *original and a bit different.***
A She chooses items that are not *too expensive* and that *most people can afford.*
C She has to send some *larger items*, so not everything is easy to carry.

24 **B Correct. She will *probably need more staff.***
A She isn't going to open a new shop.
C She thought about selling more food, but another shop selling food has just opened.

25 **A Correct. [She's] *working more hours than* [she has] *ever done and that's probably the most difficult thing.***
B She gets on well with her customers.
C She likes travelling.

Practice Test 2

Reading

Part 1 p62

1 **B Correct. Girls who wish to play football are invited to *come to the first training session next Monday evening.***

A The message is about a *new girls' team*, so it's for girls who want to play football, not watch it.

C There will be a training session, not a game, *next Monday evening*.

2 **A Correct. Passengers for *destinations in Europe* have to go to *Terminal 2*.**

B Terminal 1 is *for flights within the US only*, so passengers for anywhere else in the world cannot fly from here.

C Passengers flying to *destinations in Europe*, not America, should *follow the yellow signs*.

3 **B Correct. Rob Masters left a message that *they want to arrange an interview* and that Seiko *should call them back*.**

A Rob Masters called to *arrange an interview*, not cancel it.

C Anita took a call from Rob Masters, not Seiko, and it was about the job Seiko applied for.

4 **C Correct. *Hot meals will not be served in the college canteen until next week.***

A It's the *hot meals* service that is delayed, not the new term.

B The notice is about hot meals only, so students can still eat in the dining area e.g. their own snacks.

5 **C Correct. Luca asks Fran to *do some shopping* and says that he has *left a list*.**

A Luca says that he'll *make* [them] *something nice*, so he'll do the cooking.

B Luca talks about what he'll do when he gets *back from the library*, but he doesn't ask Fran to take anything back there.

Part 2 p64

6 **F José / Paradise Café**

needs to eat a lot of vegetables: *the carrot and spinach soup and the freshly-picked salads*

doesn't have a lot of money: *without you needing to spend too much* likes eating outside: *enjoy the summer weather in the garden*

7 **H Sarah / Jackie's Juice Bar**

chooses places where the service is fast: *great if you want a quick lunch*

likes to eat healthy food: *the salads and juices are really good for you*

loves fresh fruit and vegetables: *Everything is made from the freshest ingredients available*

8 **D Karl / The Great Castle Dining Hall**

places with good music and an interesting mood: *musicians add to the atmosphere.*

loves untypical food: *For a more unusual dining experience ... a six course meal of delicacies from* [1,000 years ago].

often enjoys going to a spectacular location by car to get something special: *drive out to this castle and eat like the rich families of 1,000 years ago*

9 **G Fernando / The Hollywood Restaurant**

a meal in a special restaurant: *a restaurant with its own cinema!*

doesn't mind about the cost: *it's not cheap once you add in the cinema tickets and the price of your meal*

must be close to the city centre: *located in the centre of the city*

10 **B Linda and Barry / Bob's Barbecue**

live music: *often a live band performs*

menu with a variety of options: *tasty fish dishes, sausages and steaks grilled on the fire and the kids' menus offer a wide choice*

are happy to pay a bit more for excellent food: *It's fantastic food, wasn't cheap*

Part 3 p66

11 **A Correct. She says that she has *always been keen on sport*, so she decided to join her *local athletics club*.**

B She says she has *always been very fit*.

C She mentions her coach, but doesn't say that she wanted to become a coach.

D She says that she started focusing on the long jump because she was good at it.

12 **A Correct. She says that in the 800 metres race you have to *choose the right moment to run at your maximum speed*.**

B She says that she does not *run the short distances like 100 metres*, so she isn't comparing the two distances.

C She says that *you have to mix speed with strength*, so they are equally important.

D *You also have to think a lot about how you race*, so you cannot forget everything.

13 **D Correct. She says she loves *running in front of a crowd – I suppose it's a sort of performance*.**

A She was nervous before her *first race*, but she isn't nervous any more because she loves *running in front of a crowd* and she has *learned to stay calm*.

B She says that she enjoys *running in front of a crowd*, but she doesn't say how it feels to be in front of other competitors in a race.

C She says that running *has helped* [her] *to trust in* [her] *own abilities*, but not that she has developed new ones.

14 **C Correct. She eats *well* but does not have a *special diet*.**

A She describes *eating more of everything* because she's so active, but she doesn't say it makes her able to run faster.

B She tries to *eat and sleep well* but she doesn't say that eating helps her to sleep better.

D She gets *plenty of variety*, so she does eat different types of food.

15 **B Correct. At first, she *put all her effort into the long jump* because it was her *best event*. She says that she loves running, but that she isn't aiming for the position of Olympic athletes because *you have to give up so much if you want to reach that level*.**

A She mentions *Olympic athletes* but says *I don't feel that is necessarily where I'm aiming*.

C She says *I love running in front of a crowd* and doesn't say that she finds training boring.

D She *trains with others*, but she doesn't mention competing in a team.

Part 4 p68

16 C 17 H 18 B 19 F 20 E

Part 5 p69

21 A currently

***Currently* is used in present continuous and it means *now*.**

Previously and *recently* aren't used in this tense, and *newly* has a wrong meaning.

22 D work

***Work as* is used with a noun to describe someone's job.**

Be, *learn* and *feel* are not used with *as* followed by a noun.

23 B preparing

***Preparing* is used to mean *making* [the lessons] *ready in advance*.**

Practising and *reading* aren't used with *lessons* in this way, and *thinking* would need to be followed by *about*.

24 C rather

***Rather* is used with *than* to mean *instead of*.**

Sooner means *earlier*. *Instead* and *even* aren't used with *than*.

25 D while

***While* is used to introduce something happening at the same time as something else.**

Throughout in this sentence would need to be followed by a noun (*throughout their studies*), not a subject and verb. *However* and *except* aren't correct in this position.

26 D way

***Way* in the expression *in this way* means *in this kind of system or method*.**

Kind and *type* aren't used in this expression. *In this style* can mean *in this way*, but doesn't fit this context for an exact plan.

Part 6 p70

27 for
28 All
29 any
30 such
31 to
32 on

Writing

Part 1 p71

Below is a model answer for Question 1 and some comments on it.

Model answer

Hi Sarah,

I'm excited about our shopping trip, too! Let's meet at the bus station.

I'd prefer to go to the new fast food restaurant for lunch. It will be more exciting than having a picnic by the river. We can see what food the new restaurant has. I hope they have burgers!

Yes, I'd like to buy a birthday present for my best friend in town. I want to buy her a cool T-shirt. She loves T-shirts.

I'd also like to buy some new earrings and a magazine in town. What do you want to do?

See you soon!

Anna

(101 words)

Comments

Anna has answered all parts of the question, and her answer is the correct length. She has used appropriate opening and closing remarks in her email, and her response is well organized and easy to understand. Anna uses different structures and appropriate vocabulary in her email and she has not made any grammatical or spelling errors.

Part 2 p72

Below is a model answer for Question 2 and some comments on it.

Model answer

I love Italian food. My favourite Italian foods are pizza and pasta. They are the best foods in the world. They are so delicious. I love all kinds of pizza and pasta. My mum is a very good cook, so I like eating at home. She can make anything, and it is as good as in a restaurant. She makes amazing pasta dishes. I enjoy eating in restaurants, too, because they have a lot of different things on the menu. I like to try new foods in restaurants. But eating at home is best because I like eating with my family.

(101 words)

Comments

This is a very good attempt. The writer answers the question and the article is the correct length. The response is well organized and easy to understand. The writer uses a good range of structures (*I love ....*, *My favourite ...*, *She makes ...*) and a range of appropriate vocabulary (*cook*, *restaurant*, *delicious*, *dishes*, *menu*). There are no grammatical or spelling errors.

Below is a model answer for Question 3 and some comments on it.

Model answer

When the postman gave me the parcel, I had no idea what was inside. It had my name and address on it, but I didn't recognize the writing. The parcel was not heavy, and it felt like a big empty box. I took the parcel into the kitchen and put it on the table. I took some scissors and carefully cut the paper open. There was a big box inside. I took off the lid and a big red balloon came out of the box. It said 'Happy Birthday!' on it. I was very surprised because it wasn't my birthday!

(100 words)

Comments

This is a good story of the correct length, which answers the question and uses the first sentence correctly. The writer uses different structures and the correct tense (*I had ...*, *The parcel was not ...*, *There was ...*). There is a range of appropriate vocabulary (*name*, *address*, *box*, *paper*, *lid*, etc.), and no grammatical or spelling errors. The story is well structured and easy to understand.

Listening

Part 1 p73

1 B Correct. The weather forecast for tomorrow is *more of the same*, which is *cloudy* with *a few showers*, although *the winds will be stronger than today*.

A It will be *cloudy* but the *sunnier weather* will not arrive until *towards the weekend*.

C The forecast was originally for *a storm* and *very heavy rain*, but the forecast has changed and so *tomorrow's weather won't be quite what was expected*.

2 C Correct. The girl says that her brother Paul has *shorter hair* than Robbie and would never wear *such smart clothes*, and he's wearing *sunglasses*.

A The girl says that her brother Paul *would never wear such smart clothes* and he's wearing *sunglasses*.

B The girl says that the boy *with long hair* is a *friend from work*.

Answer key

Answer key

3 **B Correct. The girl *used to do a lot of running and swimming*, but she *got tired of the jogging* [running] so only does swimming now. We also know she's going swimming tonight because she says she'll be *out of the pool by 7.00*.**

A The boy, not the girl, is *going to the gym*.

C The girl says she *got tired of the jogging* [running], so she doesn't do that anymore.

4 **B Correct. The woman says the club is *a fantastic place to play table tennis*.**

A *There are plans to open a café next year*, but it's not open now.

C *The Internet café closed last spring*, and computers are not mentioned as part of what is available at the club.

5 **A Correct. The man says *there's no mouse here either*, and the woman isn't surprised and promises to send one *straight away*.**

B The man can't find the keyboard at first, but then he says *here we are* so we know he's found it.

C The printer *has to be ordered separately*, so it's not missing from this order.

6 **C Correct. The boy's mother has put his money *by the front door* so that he *wouldn't forget it*.**

A *Jenny took the money from the table*, but the boy's isn't there.

B The boy says the money is *not in* [his] *jacket pocket*.

7 **B Correct. Susie's friend *found an old address book with her number in*, phoned her and *left a message*, and Susie *called* [the girl] *back*.**

A Susie *lost her mobile two weeks ago and she hasn't bought a new one yet*.

C Susie's friend sent her an *email*, but Susie didn't write any emails.

Part 2 p75

8 **B Correct. She says that the story is *difficult to follow*.**

A She says that the book is short, but it took her a long time to read it.

C She says that she had to read parts of the book again to work out what was going on.

9 **A Correct. The man says that his neighbour is a member of a lot of local clubs.**

B The man says that his neighbour *seems like a nice guy*.

C The man says that his neighbour has a job in town, but doesn't say that he works hard.

10 **A Correct. They say he's never on time.**

B The woman says that he's got an expensive watch, but he never looks at it.

C The man says that he came but was very late.

11 **C Correct. The boy says that they didn't have enough time at the museum because it took so long to get there and back.**

A The boys says that there were *interesting things* at the museum and he *found out some useful information for his history project*.

B The boy says that it took a long time to get to the museum and back.

12 **B Correct. She says that it's *really convenient to be so close to the shops and theatres*.**

A She says that the building makes noises, and that her neighbour is very friendly.

C She says that *it's always strange sleeping in a new place*.

13 **A Correct. They say that the queues are very long and the supermarket needs *more staff*.**

B They say that there is a good *selection of food*.

C They say that the prices are lower than in other supermarkets in town.

Part 3 p77

14 walking
15 600 / six hundred
16 diving
17 June
18 bus tour
19 return flights

Part 4 p78

20 **A Correct. *Just a dozen groups played*, which means 12 bands.**

B The festival began *in the early 1980s*, not the year 1980.

C The first festival *began at lunchtime and was over before it got dark*.

21 **C Correct. The festival provides a wide range of entertainment for *young and old alike*.**

A *Ticket numbers have been reduced slightly this year*, so the crowd will be smaller, not bigger.

B The festival is *a four-day event*, which is longer than a weekend.

22 **B Correct. The audience will *recognize people such as Mark Whitfield and Sandy Denver from TV*.**

A There will be some of *the best names in comedy*, but they aren't all local, a number of international stars will be appearing, too.

C US comic Joe Reen has had to cancel his appearance, so there won't be a top American entertainer.

23 **C Correct. *On Saturday and Sunday, you can watch ... videos covering the history of rock music*.**

A You can watch, not read, *a non-stop programme of music biographies*.

B You can watch thrillers on Friday night.

24 **A Correct. The presenter is particularly looking forward to buying *albums you just can't find anywhere else*.**

B The presenter mentions that you can buy *a jacket to keep the rain off*, but this is not what he's especially looking forward to.

C The presenter says it's possible to buy *a candle for a friend*, but this is not what he is especially looking forward to.

25 **B Correct. *Westbay has more food stalls from around the world than any other festival*.**

A The presenter mentions the tastes of Mexico, but doesn't say they're very hot.

C It's possible to try Australian barbecued lamb, so not everything is vegetarian.

Practice Test 3

Reading

Part 1 p82

1 **B Correct. You can use a mobile phone in the *reception* area.**
A You are permitted to use a phone in *reception*.
C You can use your mobile phone in the *reception* area; the receptionist's phone is not mentioned.

2 **C Correct. Aisha wants to know the name of the shop where David bought the book.**
A David has already lent a book to Aisha, but she's lost it.
B Aisha doesn't ask David to go into town with her.

3 **B Correct. You take the medicine *on an empty stomach*, so you can eat after you have taken the medicine.**
A You mustn't eat before taking the medicine, but it doesn't say when you should eat.
C You should take the medicine *every six hours*.

4 **C Correct. The changing rooms are for people *having tennis lessons*.**
A You should use the main changing room if you are *not* having tennis lessons.
B The notice doesn't mention the staff.

5 **C Correct. The security guard doesn't turn the lights off because people are asked to *switch off the lights* when they leave.**
A *The security guard will lock the doors.*
B You don't need to ask the security guard for permission. You should *switch off the lights when you leave*.

Part 2 p84

6 **F Lisa / Time Museum**
deciding what period of history to study: *can access timelines for specific regions with our new software.*
wants to visit a general history museum: *travel through time; starting in ancient Egypt ... ending up with most recent inventions.*

7 **E Marcus / Fun Science**
nephew is interested in space: r*ocket simulator, 3D film on stars and planets*
nephew gets bored, so needs plenty of equipment: *have fun; do experiments at the different science fun labs*

8 **A Ben and Erica / City Museum**
want their children (aged 8 and 12) to do something creative: *dinosaur drawing for children aged 4–8; for children aged 12, we have tablets with the new museum Imagine app*
want to spend time with them: p*arents please stay, you can take part in the activities, too*

9 **C Yoko / The Glass Place**
museum where she can see things being made: *watch a glass-making demonstration*
wants to buy some unusual gifts: *gift shop where you can buy amazing glass items, including jewellery*

10 **D Robert and Meg / History Museum**
want to know about history of parents: *special exhibition that explores the history of the past 100 years*
want to know about ordinary life: *[exhibition] looking at houses, schools, shops, work and developments in transport; interviews with local people*

Part 3 p86

11 **B Correct. *Most of all,* [he] *liked taking pictures of people.***
A The text doesn't say that he took pictures of his parents.
C The writer also enjoyed taking pictures of *flowers, trees and animals.*
D The writer's parents bought him a camera when he was ten years old.

12 **B Correct. The writer had to take *dull pictures of local buildings and new types of cars.***
A The writer didn't take pictures of people in his first job.
C The writer worked for a *local paper* and didn't travel far in his job.
D He had to go out of the office to take photographs.

13 **D Correct. The writer thinks that people imagine that he is *an unpleasant person.***
A The writer thinks that people imagine that he makes a lot of money.
B The writer thinks that people imagine that he takes embarrassing photos of famous people.
C The writer thinks that people imagine that he follows famous people.

14 **A Correct. The writer photographs people who ask him *to photograph them.***
B Some people imagine that the writer is an *unpleasant person who follows famous people* but the writer doesn't describe the people he photographs as unpleasant.
C The writer does feel annoyed sometimes, if people *decide that they don't want to be photographed.*
D The writer doesn't mention this as a problem.

15 **C Correct. The writer works for himself and finds his job *exciting and challenging.***
A The writer didn't enjoy his first job.
B The writer prefers taking pictures of people, but he doesn't want to embarrass people.
D The writer doesn't mention anything about wanting to be famous.

Part 4 p88

16 G 17 C 18 H 19 B 20 E

Part 5 p89

21 **trip**
***Trip* refers to a journey during which you visit a place and return.**
Destination means the place you're travelling to, *route* refers to the roads taken on the journey and *plan* means an idea or arrangement to do something in the future.

22 **routine**
Routine* completes the phrase *daily routine.
Practice, habit and *custom* aren't correct in this context.

23 **offered**
Offered* completes the phrase *to be offered the chance to do something.
Advised, recommended and *suggested* aren't used with the object *chance*.

24 **must**
***Must* is followed by the infinitive without *to*.**
Ought and *need* require *to* + infinitive; *could* indicates possibility and isn't correct in this context.

25 **somebody**
Somebody **refers to a person.**
Everyone refers to a lot of people, which isn't correct in this context; *something* and *everything* refer to things, not people.

26 **free**
Be free to **means you can decide something yourself.**
Open, *empty* and *clear* aren't correct in this context.

Part 6 p90

27 in
28 from
29 for
30 there
31 with
32 away

Writing

Part 1 p91

Below is a model answer for Question 1 and some comments on it.

Model answer

Hi Carla,

I'm really excited about the talent show, too! I'd love to be in your band! It'll be amazing!

I'm not a great singer, but I can play the guitar. I've been having lessons for two years, and I know a few songs.

I know two other people who can be in our band. My friend Anna can play the keyboards and my friend Dino is a great singer! They're good musicians.

I think we should make cool costumes for our band and wear them in the talent show. What do you think?

See you soon!

Maria

(100 words)

Comments

Maria has answered all parts of the question and her email is of the correct length. Her response is well organized and easy to understand. She has used a variety of different structures and a good range of vocabulary in her email. She has not made any grammatical or spelling errors.

Part 2 p92

Below is a model answer for Question 2 and some comments on it.

Model answer

I love listening to music. My favourite kinds of music are pop music and rock music. I like these kinds of music because they are good to dance to. I love dancing! I often listen to music on my own in my room, and I often listen to music and dance with my friends, too. I like going to concerts, but I prefer listening to music at home. There are a lot of people shouting, singing and screaming at a concert, and you can't always hear the music. I prefer to hear the music and the words to my favourite songs.

(101 words)

Comments

This is a very good attempt. The writer answers the question. Her response is well organized and easy to understand. She uses a good range of structures (*I like / love / prefer ... because ..., There are ...)* and appropriate vocabulary (*pop, rock, dance, shout, sing, scream, concert, songs*).

Below is a model answer for Question 3 and some comments on it.

Model answer

It was midnight when the telephone rang. I was asleep. I woke up and sat up in my bed. I felt shocked and surprised. Why did someone want to speak to me at this time? I went downstairs. The telephone rang and rang. I answered the phone, but there was no one there. Strange! I looked out the window at the dark night. The moon was big and bright. There were many, many stars. As I was looking, the telephone rang again. I turned quickly. There were shadows on the walls. I was frightened and I didn't know why. I answered the phone again and said hello. 'Wrong number,' said the voice. 'Sorry.'

(113 words)

Comments

This is a very good attempt. The story is atmospheric and well written. The writer has used tenses correctly (*I was asleep, As I was looking ..., I turned quickly,* etc.) and a good range of vocabulary (*shocked, surprised, strange, dark, bright, shadows,* etc.).

Listening

Part 1 p93

1 **C Correct. The woman is going to go to work although she feels ill.**
A She may go to the doctor's surgery if she can make an appointment.
B She wants to stay in bed, but she can't because she has an important meeting.

2 **C Correct. His birthday is *on Thursday*.**
A He wants to celebrate his birthday *on Tuesday*.
B He's meeting an old school friend *on Wednesday*.

3 **B Correct. They're going to go to *the park*.**
A They were invited to a house *by the sea*, but she decided not to go.
C They went to the *theme park* the previous week.

4 **A Correct. There was *flooding in the kitchens*.**
B There was *flooding in the kitchens* yesterday, not a fire.
C There was a *fire in one of the science labs* two weeks ago.

5 **B Correct. He used some *history magazines*.**
A He had a *quick look on the Internet*, but he *used some magazines*.
C He *couldn't find any good books* in the library.

6 **C Correct. The man *put them in a small bag*.**
A They are *by the front door*, not *on the bed*.
B The woman looked on the *kitchen table*, but they weren't there.

7 **A Correct. She's going to an *Italian restaurant* to celebrate.**
B The restaurant is *opposite the theatre*.
C The woman has already *been for an interview*.

Part 2 p95

8 **A Correct. They expected to find it *boring*, but it wasn't.**
B The play lasted for *nearly two hours*, but this wasn't a problem.
C The actors showed what was happening without speaking.

9 A Correct. He finds it difficult to type because the phone has tiny keys.

B The phone has a good camera.

C The phone has all the apps the man needs.

10 C Correct. The train has been *cancelled*.

A The man has already been waiting for ten minutes.

B There has been a *problem on the track*.

11 B Correct. The woman wanted to eat at eight o'clock, but their booking is for nine o'clock.

A They need to tell their friends that they're going to eat later than expected.

C She hopes *the food is worth waiting for*.

12 B Correct. The woman says that you *can't believe anything* in the newspaper.

A The man says that his newspaper is cheaper than other newspapers.

C The man jokes that the woman is very modern because she reads the news online.

13 C Correct. She says that it was wonderful and she could relax.

A The woman says that the man would have been bored.

B The woman says that she felt tired before she went on holiday, but that she feels full of energy now.

Part 3 p97

14 Introduction

15 questions

16 next to

17 200 / two hundred

18 Manager

19 Drinks

Part 4 p98

20 B The wildlife centre event is for *children aged between five and nine, and parents are asked to stay*.

A The speaker recommends a specific age group.

C The event is for children, but parents are *asked to stay*.

21 C The organizers may continue the club *in term time*.

A *Young people bring their music to the club.*

B This is a *new club*.

22 B Drinks *will be provided*.

A The children go home for lunch.

C The children take their own snacks.

23 C Children *learn new steps and routines*.

A Parents see what the children have learned but don't take part themselves.

B The Dance Academy teaches a variety of styles, not only modern dance.

24 B The club is on *twice a week* in the holidays.

A This is not different in the holidays.

C There will be *all the usual activities*, and there isn't more sport than usual.

25 B There's *an open day* and *everything is free*.

A *Everything is free*, so it doesn't cost anything.

C Children can try everything that is available at the centre.

Practice Test 4

Reading

Part 1 p102

1 **C Correct. The *changes to the timetable* relate to *information about the exams* and students can get this *from the office*.**

A There have been *some changes to the timetable* so it can't be *the same as it was before*.

B There have been *changes to the timetable*, but the students don't need to tell anyone about them. They should *visit the office*, but to *get a new copy*.

2 **B Correct. You don't pay a delivery charge if the order is *over £15*, but if it's less, *you'll need to pay*.**

A You do have to pay for delivery if the order is less than £15, but the text doesn't say how much the delivery costs.

C All food is delivered, but if you spend more than £15 on food, you don't have to pay for delivery.

3 **C Correct. Jaime wants to meet at the restaurant instead of Lucia's house, so he's changing their arrangements.**

A Jaime wants to *meet at the restaurant* so he isn't cancelling the evening, he's changing the meeting place.

B Jaime wants to meet on the same evening, so he doesn't want to *postpone* the meal.

4 **B Correct. The dining room *is closed* which means nobody can use it.**

A The dining room is closed for the next *two weeks*, so it isn't possible to use it *next week*.

C There's *building work* in the *staff dining room*, which means nobody at all can use it for dining.

5 **C Correct. Tess wants to *get something together on the Internet*, which means she wants to share the cost of a present.**

A Tess wants to buy a present *with* Lenny on *the Internet* for their *mum*.

B Tess has already been to town and *couldn't find anything* so she doesn't want to meet Lenny in town.

Part 2 p104

6 **E Jake / How It Began**

enjoys watching fast-moving and entertaining films: *an exciting and original story that you won't be able to stop watching*

he'd like to watch something really up to date: *movie has only just been released*

7 **H Mara / Across The World: A Three-part Series**

enjoys watching international sport: *topics which include European football, South American football*

interested in its history: *all-time greats*

would like a good balance of talk and play: *includes interviews; highlights of every World Cup Final so far*

loves listening to famous stars talking: *The series includes interviews with all-time greats*

8 **A Harry / Changing Direction**

is a film student / is interested in the history of film: *watch the secrets of directors Spielberg, Tarantino, Hitchcock and more*

how film has developed over the years: *Learn ... how they changed the path of film-making forever*

see something about the early film industry / the latest technology: *[it] compares the equipment directors used ... with what they use today*

9 **B Natalia / A Fascinating Story**

enjoys watching serious documentaries: *an amazing look at the secret life of the snow leopard / filming is excellent and the narration is fascinating*

keen to understand more about the natural world: *find out about the snow leopards' habits, how they're threatened and what is being done to save them*

interested in the variety of different plants and animals in different regions around the world and what can be done to protect them: *learn about the latest conservation programmes that the Biodiversity Trust is working on*

10 **D Chan / The Best Of: *What's New?***

likes to find out about current affairs: *programme which checks people's knowledge of the news*

would prefer something light that can make him laugh: *an extremely funny programme; picks out the funniest moments*

Part 3 p106

11 **A Correct. Mark *has taken photos of all kinds of amazing weather, including tornadoes, thunderstorms and hurricanes*.**

B Mark is the author of several books. There's no mention of his photos being used in books.

C Mark has appeared in documentaries, but there's no mention of his photos being used in documentaries.

D Mark has written articles about our changing weather, but there's no mention of his photos changing over time.

12 **B Correct. *Mark has also successfully appeared in documentaries on American TV to discuss severe weather*.**

A Mark has written *a very popular blog about extreme weather.*

C Mark has written *fascinating articles* about *our changing weather*.

D He has *appeared in documentaries on American TV* and he's a *keen speaker.*

13 **B Correct. Mark enjoyed *recording the sound effects of weather*.**

A He had a camera, but he was *more interested in recording the sound effects of weather*.

C Mark *never forgot* seeing his first hurricane. There's no mention that he was *afraid of severe storms*.

D Mark *never forgot* seeing *his first hurricane*. There's no mention of him being hurt.

14 **B Correct. He *began his career as a writer* working on local newspapers and *he was good at his job*.**

A He *studied journalism* and *he never regretted that he'd become a journalist*.

C He wrote for *local newspapers*, but he didn't take *photographs*.

D He became an artist in terms of *photography*, but we don't know whether he was a better artist than a journalist.

15 **C Correct. The writer describes aspects of Mark's *career* as a *photographer* from his childhood interest to his adult career.**

A The writer talks about Mark's career as a photographer, but doesn't *give advice* on how to become one.

B The writer talks about Mark's career as a photographer, but doesn't *encourage* people to become one.

D There's no technical explanation of *how to take photos* in the text.

Part 4 p108

16 G **17** A **18** D **19** F **20** B

Part 5 p109

21 idea

***Idea* in this context means *the first time something is thought of*.**

Aim, *plan* and *view* don't have the correct meaning in this context.

22 where

***Where* is a relative pronoun that is used with places.**

We use *what* and *which* with things, and *who* with people.

23 take

***Take* is used in the expression *take part*, which means *to join in with something*.**

Get, *have* and *make* aren't used in this expression.

24 keen

***Keen* is followed by the preposition *on*.**

Attracted is followed by *by*. *Interested* is followed by *in*. *Happy* is followed by *with*.

25 should

***Should* is the correct modal for recommending or giving advice about something.**

Need is followed by *to* + infinitive. *Ought* is followed by *to*. *Would* is used in conditional sentences.

26 way

***Way* is used in the expression *in this way* to mean *like this*.**

Course, *direction* and *route* aren't used in this expression.

Part 6 p110

27 around
28 in
29 why
30 on
31 out
32 everyone / everybody

Writing

Part 1 p111

Below is a model answer for Question 1 and some comments on it.

Model answer

Hi Ben,

I can't wait to come and visit you next weekend. I'm looking forward to meeting your family.

The museum in your town sounds interesting, but I'd prefer to go to the beach for a picnic on Saturday. It'll be fun to play in the sea and relax on the beach.

I'd love to watch a film at the cinema on Sunday. I like action films and comedy films. I hope we like the same kinds of films!

Is there a souvenir shop in your town? I'd like to buy a gift for my mum!

See you soon!

Carlos

(101 words)

Comments

Carlos has answered all parts of the question, and his email is the correct length. His response is well organized and easy to understand. He has used a lot of different structures (*I'd prefer ..., There isn't ..., I like / enjoy ..., I hope ...*, etc.) and a good range of vocabulary in his email. He has made no grammatical or spelling errors.

Part 2 p112

Below is a model answer for Question 2 and some comments on it.

Model answer

I love sightseeing holidays best of all. I like visiting interesting cities and seeing all the historical buildings and interesting places. I love visiting new places because it's always good to see new things and learn about life in other places. I usually go on holiday with my family. We go to an island with beautiful beaches and a lot of good restaurants. I like beach holidays, but I'd prefer to visit a big city. My dream holiday is a trip to New York. I want to see all the famous landmarks there and walk in Central Park.

(98 words)

Comments

This is a very good attempt. The writer answers the question. Her response is well organized and easy to understand. She uses a good range of structures (*I love ..., I like visiting ..., because ..., ... I'd prefer to ...*) and appropriate vocabulary (*sightseeing, cities, historical buildings, island, beaches, restaurants, landmarks*). There are no grammatical or spelling errors.

Below is a model answer for Question 3 and some comments on it.

Model answer

When I woke up, it was raining. I was disappointed because I wanted to go to the beach. I phoned my friend and my friend came to my house. We sat in my room and we listened to music. Then the rain stopped. We were very happy. We ran to the station and took a train to the beach. Now the sun was shining and it was lovely and warm. We had fun on the beach and we met some interesting people. We decided to meet again the next weekend. I was glad that the rain had stopped because I had a perfect day.

(104 words)

Comments

This is a very good attempt. The writer answers the question and uses the initial sentence correctly. His response is well organized and easy to understand. He uses the correct tenses and a good range of structures (*We sat ..., ... the sun was shining ..., I was glad that ... because ...*). He uses a range of vocabulary and a good selection of adjectives (*disappointed, happy, lovely, interesting, glad, perfect*). There are no grammatical or spelling errors.

Listening

Part 1 p113

1 C Correct. The boy says that the orange juice was *OK* so he must have had some to drink.

A The girl asked about the *coffee*, but the boy doesn't *drink coffee*.

B The boy says that he *usually* has a *milkshake*, but that the café doesn't sell it.

2 C Correct. There's a separate book-signing event with Karabo on the *25th*.

A Tickets for both can be purchased from the *21st*.

B She'll be reading from her latest novel, *Philo and Burke*, at 7 p.m. on April *24th*.

Answer key

3 **C Correct. The woman took a job in *a music shop in town* and says *it's about the same money* as her last job, so we know she still works there.**

A The woman *left* her job in the cinema *about a month ago*.

B The woman *started working* in a *supermarket* but left because it was so *boring*.

4 **B Correct. Although the day of the exam has changed, the time of the exam *remains* the *same*. It's still *nine o'clock*.**

A You have to get there half an hour before the exam, which is *8.30*, but the time of the exam remains the same, at *nine o'clock*.

C The *French* exam is at *one o'clock*.

5 **C Correct. Sara has got *dark hair* which is *long* and she *ties it back*.**

A Sara has got *long dark hair*, but she *ties it back*.

B Sara has got *long* dark hair.

6 **B Correct. The man is meeting his friends in the *new burger place*.**

A The woman is going to the cinema, not the man.

C The man is going to town, but he isn't *going shopping*. The woman is going shopping.

7 **C Correct. The girl put the magazine on her *desk* and it's *on top of* her *English book*.**

A The magazine was in her bag, but the girl *took it out of there*.

B The magazine is *on top of* the English book, not underneath it.

Part 2 p115

8 **B Correct. She thinks the woman is feeling *calm*.**

A The man thinks the woman in the painting looks *sad*.

C She thinks the woman in the painting looks *as though she's just realized the answer to a difficult problem*.

9 **C Correct. She says that she can't *remember which pocket* [she's] *put things in*.**

A She says that *it's bigger* than her old bag.

B She says that she bought it because it has a lot of pockets.

10 **B Correct. He says that he wishes he could *get it out of* [his] *head*.**

A He says that he hears it all the time.

C He says that he can't stop singing it.

11 **C Correct. He says that the water in the pool was *freezing*.**

A The woman says that the pool was very busy on Saturday.

B The woman says that there was hardly any room to swim on Saturday because the pool was so busy.

12 **B Correct. She says that it was *wonderful to breathe clean air after all the pollution in the city*.**

A She says there isn't much light from cars in the countryside.

C She says that there isn't much light from buildings in the countryside.

13 **A Correct. He ate *far more than* [he] *needed*.**

B He says that he doesn't want to get too comfortable in case he falls asleep.

C He says that he ate *two helpings*, but couldn't manage a third.

Part 3 p117

14 13th / thirteenth
15 Park
16 6 / six
17 extreme cycling
18 map
19 team

Part 4 p118

20 **A Correct. He wants to show that exploring is something *all young people can take part in*.**

B The presenter says that it isn't only for the *super fit and super confident*, it's for *all young people*.

C David is a *leader*, but he's keen for young people to *take part* in expeditions, not to learn how to become leaders.

21 **C Correct. Youth Expeditions work with *environmentalists* and want *people who are keen to learn*.**

A Youth Expeditions provide a grant for about *75%*. The young people pay the rest.

B Youth Expeditions *don't expect them* [young people] *to have expert scientific knowledge already*.

22 **B Correct. The summer expeditions take place in *the Arctic*.**

A The summer expeditions are for young people *aged 16–20*.

C The expeditions are *month-long*.

23 **A Correct. They investigated *glaciers, rivers, plants*, which is the *geography of the area*.**

B They *cross-country skied* to get to their destination, but they didn't do any *adventure sports*.

C They went camping, but not *without their leaders*.

24 **B Correct. There will be *opportunities for mountaineering and cross-country skiing*.**

A *Three young explorers can win* the competition.

C They will study *climate change for part of the time*.

25 **C Correct. They make a short film about *themselves* and say *why they are interested in going to the Arctic*.**

A They make a film about *themselves*, not *about the Arctic*.

B They must say what they hope to *get out of the experience*, but they don't have to describe any *previous experience of exploring*.

Practice Test 5

Reading

Part 1 p122

1 **A Correct. If you wish to do art classes next month, you should tell the teacher *by 30th April.***

B You should *go to Room 58* to *tell Paul Davidson* that you wish to *do art classes*; we don't know where the art classes are taking place.

C You should see Mr Davidson to tell him you wish to *do art classes*, which have not started yet.

2 **C Correct. Michael asks Ruby to *ask Dave to wait for* [him] *at the airport* because the plane lands after the time of the last train into town.**

A Michael asks Ruby to *ask* Dave, which means give a message to Dave, not to take him or Dave anywhere.

B Dave cannot catch the 10.45 p.m. train because his plane doesn't arrive until 11.30 p.m.

3 **C Correct. Gerry is asking Paula to *make sure the cats have enough water* while he's away.**

A Gerry, not Paula, is coming back on Monday. Also, it's Paula who must check *the cats have enough water* while Gerry is away.

B There's a *yellow bowl under the sink*, so Paula doesn't need to buy one.

4 **A Correct. Drivers should be careful not to park *near the crossroads* because *long vehicles may be turning* there.**

B The notice is warning other drivers about *long vehicles*, not telling lorry drivers where to park.

C The notice doesn't say anything about parking cars close to each other, only about parking *near the crossroads*.

5 **B Correct. Photos and several banknotes have been *found in* [a] *shop*, so the manager thinks they have been lost there.**

A The contact number is for the manager, not the owner of the wallet.

C The manager has *found* the pictures, not taken them.

Part 2 p124

6 **D Joe / Aim For The Stars**

interested in films about true, historic events: *about the very first people to fly to the moon*

his favourites are about well-known people, especially those whose lives were changed by their experiences: *it looks into the lives of some of the people involved in this important event, particularly Buzz Aldrin, the second man to step onto the moon's surface, there's enough drama in it to keep most people interested, the last part of the film is quite unexpected*

7 **G Sandra / The Island**

love stories: *a romantic movie*

doesn't mind unhappy endings: *feels the sadness of the conclusion*

actors must be really good: *what's special about this film is the quality of the acting*

8 **F Dimitri / Down On The Farm**

doesn't like films that are complicated: *the story is always easy to understand*

enjoys watching films about life in the countryside: *learns to race horses on her parents' farm*

films that show the joys and difficulties of family life: *the relationship between Winona and her strict father is the central topic*

9 **B Danielle / Stealing By Numbers**

especially keen on films set in the last century: *story from the past, in the 1930s*

usually chooses to watch action films: *a classic adventure story, a series of dramatic adventures*

really enjoys a surprise ending: *a film that will keep you guessing until the final scene*

10 **A Maria / The Long Journey**

likes movies that make her think: *there's a real message to this movie*

filmed in a beautiful location: *you'll see a lot of the wild countryside*

an exciting story: *Plenty of drama to enjoy*

Part 3 p126

11 **D Correct. Buddy says that *people hire* [him] *when they need a musician*, and he doesn't work *for a particular band*.**

A He says that other people *hire* him, which means that they pay him to work with them, so he doesn't pay them.

B He doesn't have his own band, he works for other bands *when they need a musician*.

C He doesn't work *on* [his] *own*, he works for other bands *when they need a musician*.

12 **B Correct. He says that a session musician has to *be able to play a lot of different musical styles*.**

A A session musician has to *learn parts very quickly*, so there isn't much time to learn.

C A session musician is *in the background* and has to be prepared to *let somebody else be admired*.

D A session musician needs to be flexible about attending rehearsals *at specific times* or *at short notice*, but there's no mention of the rehearsals being long.

13 **D Correct. The writer says that there's plenty of variety in his work.**

A The writer says that he sometimes goes on a tour. He doesn't say whether he likes it or not.

B The writer says that he might work on a whole album with a band, not that he wants to record his own album.

C The writer says that he sometimes works with top bands or famous singers.

14 **B Correct. He says that his *main income has always been from studio work*, which means making recordings.**

A He says that if an album he's worked on *sells a million copies*, the band is paid well, but he isn't given *a big cheque*.

C He says that it's *fairly good money*, but that he's never been given *a big cheque*.

D He says that session musicians *generally get paid the same amount* as each other.

15 **A Correct. He says that *there's plenty of variety in this work* and that *you have to let someone else be admired*.**

B He doesn't mention appearing on television.

C He says that sometimes he *plays guitar for a top band* or goes *on a long tour with a famous singer*, but that he earns *fairly good money* for all the work he does, and never gets *a big cheque*.

D He does *play a lot of different musical styles*, but he doesn't mention playing different instruments.

Part 4 p128

16 D **17** H **18** B **19** C **20** F

Answer key

Part 5 p129

21 **However**

***However* is used to introduce a comment that contrasts with what went before.**

Whenever means *every time something happens*. *Alike* and *Ago* cannot be used to begin a sentence.

22 **need**

***Need to* + infinitive means *have to do something*.**

Must, *should* and *can* don't take *to* before the verb.

23 **says**

We use *it says* to refer to the words written on something.

Puts, *writes* and *talks* are all actions carried out by a person. The subject of the missing verb is *it*, not a person.

24 **main**

***The main ingredient* in a food product is the one that's there in the 'largest amount'.**

Main works like a superlative here (i.e. *the biggest*), but *great*, *large* and *big* don't work because they aren't in superlative form.

25 **regular**

If you eat at *regular times* of the day, you eat at similar times each day.

Common, *equal* and *even* cannot be used with this meaning.

26 **that**

Action clause *[learn when your body needs food]* + *so that* + result clause *[you don't suddenly feel the need to ...]*.

So + *what* and *so* + *when* aren't followed directly by a result clause. *So* + *which* + subject (*you*) of a clause isn't possible.

Part 6 p130

27 well
28 to
29 about
30 more
31 all
32 without

Writing

Part 1 p131

Below is a model answer for Question 1 and some comments on it.

Model answer

Hi Peter,

I hope you're very happy in your new house. Since I last emailed you, I've made a new friend at college. His name is Dan. He's a new student in my class and he's very funny.

I've been thinking about ideas for your new hobby. What about joining a sports team? You can exercise, make friends and have fun at the same time! My hobbies are playing football and swimming. I love swimming!

I'm going to watch a film at the cinema this weekend. I can't wait! Have a great time with your grandparents!

Write soon!

Harry

(101 words)

Comments

Harry has answered all parts of the question, and his email is the correct length. His response is well organized and easy to understand. He has used different tenses and structures (*I hope ..., Since I last emailed ..., I've been thinking ..., I'm going to watch ...*, etc.) and a good range of vocabulary in his email. He has made no grammatical or spelling errors.

Part 2 p132

Below is a model answer for Question 2 and some comments on it.

Model answer

I enjoy basketball and swimming. I play basketball with my local team twice a week, and I often play with my friends in the evenings or at weekends. I go swimming a lot in the summer because I live near the sea. I love swimming in the sea!

I watch basketball and football on TV. I enjoy watching my favourite teams play important matches. I prefer playing sports to watching sports because it's more fun. You can spend time with your friends and exercise, too. I think playing sports is a great way to spend your free time.

(98 words)

Comments

This is a very good attempt. The writer answers the question and his article is of the correct length. The article is well organized and easy to understand. The writer uses a good range of structures (*I enjoy ..., I often play ..., I prefer playing ..., I think ...*) and a good selection of appropriate vocabulary (*team, exercise, matches, basketball, swimming*). There are no grammatical or spelling errors.

Below is a model answer for Question 3 and some comments on it.

Model answer

Sally was pleased because at last the special day had arrived. It was her first day at college. She was excited, but also nervous, because she didn't know anyone at the college and it was bigger than her school. She went into the classroom, but she didn't know where to sit and there were so many new people! Then a girl said 'Hello' to her and asked her to sit beside her. Her name was Susan. Sally was very happy to have a new friend on her first day. Susan told her the names of the other girls in class and they were all friendly. It was a good day!

(114 words)

Comments

This is a very good attempt. The writer answers the question. Her response is well organized and easy to understand. She uses the correct tenses and a good range of structures (*It was ..., she didn't know ..., Susan told ...*) There is a good use of adjectives (*excited, nervous, happy, friendly*) and no grammatical or spelling errors.

Listening

Part 1 p133

1 **C Correct. The woman is going on the 25th, a week later than she was first planning to go.**

A The woman is going on holiday for *ten days*, not on the 10th.

B The woman was *planning to leave then* [the 18th], *but* [her] *cousin's having a big party* on that day, so they're going on the Friday after that [the 25th].

2 **B Correct. The boy *only realized it was on* when he saw *last Sunday's newspaper*.**

A The boy says the girl should *have a look at the website* in order to decide what to *get tickets for*.

C It was the girl, not the boy, who saw *an ad on TV*.

3 **A Correct. The boy asks the girl to *get* [him] *some eggs* and *a lemon*.**

B The boy is going to do *something different to* [his] *usual chocolate cake*.

C The girl is going to buy *some milk*, not the boy, and the boy doesn't need flour because he has *plenty*.

4 **C Correct. The bookshop is *left at the crossroads*, and *down a small side turning* with the *museum on the corner*.**

A You have to turn left, not right, at *the crossroads*.

B The bookshop is *down a small side turning* which is *a little way* after the crossroads, not at the crossroads.

5 **B Correct. The new neighbours have *a daughter* and an *older girl* living with them.**

A The new neighbours have two daughters living with them, not one.

C The new neighbours have three kids, *but one's already left home*.

6 **A Correct. The new houses will *be surrounded by green fields*.**

B The coast is *a short train ride away*, so we know that the new houses aren't beside the sea.

C It's possible to *get to the city in less than half an hour*, so the new houses aren't in the city.

7 **B Correct. The girl thinks that the *blue dress* is *much better than trousers*.**

A The boy says the girl could *just wear jeans and a T-shirt if* [she] *wanted*, but she's already decided that wearing a dress is a *brilliant idea*.

C The girl *was planning to wear dark jeans with a black shirt*, but she's worried that's not *smart enough* and so decides to wear a dress instead.

Part 2 p135

8 **A Correct. He says that [he doesn't] *know where* [she] *meets so many people*.**

B The woman jokes that she's good company.

C He says that he's very shy.

9 **C Correct. He wants to experience how the locals live.**

A He says that he *can't stand lying on the beach*.

B He says that he wants to *escape from the city*.

10 **A Correct. He thinks his grandma used a secret ingredient.**

B He wonders if *the measurements in the recipe are wrong*, but decides that this is not the case.

C He says that he's *followed all the instructions*, so he can't have added the ingredients in the wrong order.

11 **B Correct. The woman says that the lockers are always *taken*.**

A The man says that *there are enough machines for everyone*.

C The man says that the gym is *clean and smart*.

12 **B Correct. She likes having items of clothing which nobody else has got.**

A She says that *it's often just as expensive* to make your own clothes as it's to buy clothes in a shop.

C She doesn't say that she doesn't like buying clothes in the shops.

13 **C Correct. He can't wait for the next series to start because of the way this series ended.**

A He says that he'll have to *wait months* to find out what happened next.

B He's frustrated that something exciting or terrible is about to happen, and he doesn't know what it will be.

Part 3 p137

14 history
15 other sweets
16 January
17 8 / eight
18 10 / ten
19 bag

Part 4 p138

20 **C Correct. Paul says that he *tried a few other things* before going to work in a restaurant.**

A Paul *got a job as a kitchen assistant*, not as a chef.

B Paul worked in *the local supermarket*, but he doesn't say he opened a shop.

21 **B Correct. He says that the work was *hard* and *dirty*, but *the top chefs were highly skilled* and that he could *watch and learn*. He was also *fascinated by all the equipment*.**

A He says that *the pay wasn't great*, and also that he could *watch and learn* from the chefs.

C He says that the stories of *people injuring themselves were unlikely*.

22 **C Correct. He started *when the kitchen got busy, around twelve o'clock*.**

A His working day *sometimes wouldn't finish until two o'clock*.

B He sometimes finished, not started, work at *two o'clock the next morning* [in the early morning].

23 **A Correct. His job involves *selecting and training staff*.**

B His job involves *preparing the menus*, but he doesn't mention ordering the food.

C He says he doesn't *have to do it* [cook] *every day*.

24 **B Correct. He says that you *have to be able to work in a team*.**

A He mentions *cleaning the floor* as an example of working *in a team*, but he doesn't say that doing this makes a good chef.

C He says you *have to be able to think quickly*, not to cook quickly.

25 **A Correct. He says that *the key to success is to buy the best and the freshest food available*.**

B He says *there's a lot to think about and* [his] *work needs to be right every time* (not the customer).

C He says that the job, not the meals, can be *complicated* because *there's a lot to think about*, but that it's important to *keep things* [preparing food] *simple*.

Answer key

Practice Test 6

Reading

Part 1 p142

1 **C Correct. You can ask for information about the climbing and diving courses *at reception*.**
A They don't need a new receptionist.
B *Spaces are available*, so the courses aren't full.

2 **C Correct. The stairs can be used by anyone in *an emergency*.**
A The stairs aren't only for the emergency services.
B Customers are allowed to use the stairs, but only when there's an emergency.

3 **A Correct. Charlie tells Victoria that Jane will give her the book today.**
B Charlie doesn't need the book – he borrowed it for Victoria.
C Charlie isn't going to the lesson, but the lesson hasn't been cancelled.

4 **A Correct. People who want a locker should see Jan Harper about it.**
B People should see Jan Harper *before Friday*.
C New lockers can be reserved *before Friday*, not from Friday.

5 **B Correct. The message tells Isabel to start the meeting *without Sam*, because he's going to be late.**
A Sam doesn't want to change the day.
C The meeting is going to start at the same time.

Part 2 p144

6 **G Lynn / *Update***
looking for new places to go: *all events from clubs, pubs, leisure centres, cinemas, restaurants ...*

7 **B Tom / *Starter***
interested in unusual and exciting sports: *motocross riders, skydivers, rock climbers*
wants to know the best events in his area: *full guide to all the best competitions and other activities going on across Britain*
to get an idea of ticket costs: *everything you need to know for each sports event, venue, prices*

8 **E Jack and Hannah / *New Perspectives***
thinking of giving up jobs and starting their own business abroad: *special article giving advice to other people*
want to read about other people's experiences: *three couples who have changed their lives by moving somewhere completely new*
get useful tips on how best to do it: *practical ideas so that your move goes smoothly*

9 **H Maria / *Sparkles***
enjoys reading about celebrities: *news about all your favourite stars*
pictures of actors and pop artists at special events: *best photos, best stories, a top interview*

10 **D Ben and Maggie / *Focus***
want to read about what's going on in the world: *serious stories in the news*

Part 3 p146

11 **B Correct. She moved to Spain because she and her husband *loved Spanish culture*, and her husband wanted to paint *the Spanish countryside*.**
A They already knew that they loved the Spanish culture.
C They'd spent many holidays in Spain before moving there.
D She gave up her job in London in order to move to Spain.

12 **C Correct. The couple were ready to leave London in *just three months*.**
A They sold their home more quickly than they thought.
B The text doesn't mention this.
D They sold their house and found a house to rent for themselves.

13 **B Correct. When they arrived, they *were amazed to realize immediately that they wanted to stay longer than a year*.**
A She didn't get a teaching job on the first day.
C The owners *showed them around* and *cooked [them] a lovely meal*.
D Nobody was living in the house.

14 **B Correct. A lot of *tourists bought paintings*.**
A They sold the first picture *after two days*.
C They didn't sell any paintings on the first day.
D The shop became *very quiet* in November, after the tourists had gone home.

15 **C Correct. The writer is very positive about the move, and nothing bad has happened to them.**
A The gallery is *a great success*, so they don't regret renting it.
B They don't want to move back home because they feel they're *living a perfect life*.
D The writer never mentions missing family and friends.

Part 4 p148

16 C 17 H 18 E 19 B 20 F

Part 5 p149

21 **have**
***Have* is followed by *to* + infinitive and expresses obligation.**
Must, *should* and *might* are followed by the infinitive without *to*.

22 **instead**
***Instead* completes the phrase *instead of*, to express an alternative.**
Enough of doesn't express an alternative. *Else* and *well* aren't followed by *of*.

23 **if**
***If* links the clauses to express a conditional.**
Whether, *as* and *that* aren't used to link conditional clauses.

24 **at**
***Look at* means *examine*.**
Look on means *watch something happen*. *With* doesn't go with *look*. *Look for* means *search*.

25 **Finally**
***Finally* introduces a final point.**
Conclusion, *End* and *Last* aren't correct in this context; the phrases would be: *In conclusion*, *In the end*, *Lastly*.

26 **any**

Any **is used with an uncountable noun after a negative verb.**

Many and *various* are used with a countable noun. *Some* isn't used with a negative verb.

Part 6 p150

27 the
28 few
29 about
30 get
31 out
32 tell

Writing

Part 1 p151

Below is a model answer for Question 1 and some comments on it.

Model answer

Hi Gina,

Thanks for your email. I had a great weekend, thank you. I went to the cinema with my friend. We watched a new action film. It was great!

I enjoy reading detective stories. I like trying to guess who the criminal is! Recently, I've read the Sherlock Holmes books. They're great. My favourite book is *The Hound of the Baskervilles*. I'm sure your local library will have it. Let me know if you like it!

I really want to come and visit you soon! I could come in June. What do you think?

Write soon!

Anna

(100 words)

Comments

Anna has answered all parts of the question, and her email is the correct length. Her response is well organized and easy to understand. She has used a lot of different tenses and structures (*I had ..., I went ..., I watched ..., I've read ..., I could come ...*, etc.) and a good range of vocabulary in her email. She has not made any grammatical or spelling errors.

Part 2 p152

Below is a model answer for Question 2 and some comments on it.

Model answer

I think it's important to keep fit. You need to have a healthy body so that you can work and play and have fun. I keep fit by walking to school every day, and I also play volleyball with my friends every week. I sometimes go swimming at the weekend, too. You don't have to go to a gym or do a sport to keep fit. You can go for a walk, or dance, or do any activity that you enjoy. I think that the best way to keep fit is to do something you like because then you'll do it a lot!

(105 words)

Comments

This is a very good attempt. The writer answers the question and her article is the correct length. Her response is well organized and easy to understand. She uses a good range of structures (*I think it's ..., You need to have ..., I also play ..., You don't have to ...*, etc.) and a variety of appropriate vocabulary (*healthy, body, volleyball, swimming, gym, sport, walk, dance, activity*). There are no grammatical or spelling errors.

Below is a model answer for Question 3 and some comments on it.

Model answer

It was the worst journey I had ever been on. My family and I were on a ferry from England to France and the weather was really terrible. The sky was dark and the sea was wild, with huge waves crashing against the ferry. People were feeling awful and miserable, and many people were ill. We couldn't stand or walk because the boat was moving so much. We found a quiet place to sit. We wished we had stayed at home. Just then, the storm ended. The sea was calm and the sun came out. We arrived in France, and we were very glad that the terrible journey was over.

(110 words)

Comments

This is a very good attempt. The writer answers the question. His response is well organized and easy to understand. He uses the correct tenses and a good range of structures (*... the weather was ..., People were feeling ..., We couldn't ..., We wished ...*, etc.). The story contains a variety of adjectives (*terrible, wild, awful, miserable, ill, quiet, calm*) and no grammatical or spelling errors.

Listening

Part 1 p153

1 **B Correct. The man suggests buying *a scarf*.**
A The woman has already bought *a bag*.
C The woman is thinking about buying *a book*, but the man recommends buying *a scarf*.

2 **A Correct. Sarah *left work at six* o'clock.**
B She caught the train *at eight o'clock*.
C She got home *at nine o'clock*.

3 **C Correct. The woman is going to *have a picnic* with some friends.**
A They'd planned to go to a restaurant, but they changed the plan.
B The woman was going to make dinner at home, but she changed the plan.

4 **A Correct. It's going to rain in the afternoon.**
B *No thunderstorms are expected.*
C It will be *sunny* in the morning.

5 **C Correct. The man's friend *emailed* him about the play.**
A He *didn't* see the reviews in the newspaper.
B His *friend* heard about the play *on the radio*.

6 **B Correct. The *first* lesson is *on the 21st*.**
A The lessons *were going to start on the 15th, but the teacher was ill.*
C The *second* lesson is *on the 23rd*.

7 **A Correct. The woman usually goes *to the gym* to exercise.**
B She's running at the moment because the gym is closed.
C She hasn't *got a bike*, so she doesn't cycle.

Part 2 p155

8 **C Correct. He says that he *relies on the weather app on* [his] *phone*.**
A The woman doesn't think weather forecasts are accurate.
B The man doesn't mention that he enjoys wet weather.

9 C Correct. She says that she would *need to have a lot more money in the bank* to pursue her dream.

A She says that she'll probably continue *working in the city for a few more years.*

B She says that you *can't guarantee* that you'll make enough money as an artist.

10 B Correct. They decide to ask David to drive them to the airport.

A They decide not to leave their car at the airport while they are on holiday because it's expensive.

C They decide not to take a train to the airport because they might miss the flight if the train is delayed.

11 A Correct. He says that the biggest danger is that a firefighter won't be *fit enough* to do the job.

B He says that he isn't in dangerous situations every day.

C He says that it's important to communicate well with the rest of the team.

12 C Correct. She feels annoyed when the products get moved to new places.

A She doesn't say whether she likes buying clothes in the supermarket.

B She says that the supermarket *almost always* has all the things she needs.

13 B Correct. She says that *the characters look like people* in a film.

A The boy says that he gets bored when he can't move on to the next part of the story.

C She says that she wouldn't want the puzzles to be too easy.

Part 3 p157

14 front
15 7 / seven
16 music
17 local
18 Thursday
19 5 / five minutes

Part 4 p158

20 B Correct. People have heard a lot about the leisure centre because it's been written about *in the local newspapers*.

A There are *several leisure centres in this area.*

C There's a gym but this isn't the reason why the centre is popular.

21 C Correct. They're going to build *a fun pool with slides for children*.

A There are already two swimming pools.

B There's already a *diving area.*

22 B Correct. The manager is going to *employ more staff* for the gym.

A He doesn't mention buying more equipment.

C They aren't going to increase the number of hours that the gym is open, but they want to increase the number of hours that experienced staff are available in the gym.

23 C Correct. The centre already has indoor courts, and the *outdoor tennis courts* will be available next week.

A An outdoor basketball court isn't mentioned.

B There's already a court for volleyball.

24 B Correct. The scuba-diving courses are given by *instructors from the local diving school.*

A Most of the swimming instructors have done the course.

C The manager has done the course.

25 B Correct. The membership is cheaper than other leisure centres.

A Other leisure centres sell healthy food, too.

C Other centres also offer discounts.

Sample answer sheets

Draft

OFFICE USE ONLY - DO NOT WRITE OR MAKE ANY MARK ABOVE THIS LINE

Cambridge Assessment English

Candidate Name		Candidate Number	
Centre Name		Centre Number	
Examination Title		Examination Details	
Candidate Signature		Assessment Date	

Supervisor: If the candidate is ABSENT or has WITHDRAWN shade here ○

Preliminary Reading Candidate Answer Sheet

Instructions
Use a PENCIL (B or HB)
Rub out any answer you want to change with an eraser.

For Parts 1, 2, 3, 4 and 5:
Mark ONE letter for each answer.
For example: If you think A is the right answer to the question, mark your answer sheet like this:

Part 1

1	A ○	B ○	C ○
2	A ○	B ○	C ○
3	A ○	B ○	C ○
4	A ○	B ○	C ○
5	A ○	B ○	C ○

Part 2

6	A ○	B ○	C ○	D ○	E ○	F ○	G ○	H ○
7	A ○	B ○	C ○	D ○	E ○	F ○	G ○	H ○
8	A ○	B ○	C ○	D ○	E ○	F ○	G ○	H ○
9	A ○	B ○	C ○	D ○	E ○	F ○	G ○	H ○
10	A ○	B ○	C ○	D ○	E ○	F ○	G ○	H ○

Part 3

11	A ○	B ○	C ○	D ○
12	A ○	B ○	C ○	D ○
13	A ○	B ○	C ○	D ○
14	A ○	B ○	C ○	D ○
15	A ○	B ○	C ○	D ○

Part 4

16	A ○	B ○	C ○	D ○	E ○	F ○	G ○	H ○
17	A ○	B ○	C ○	D ○	E ○	F ○	G ○	H ○
18	A ○	B ○	C ○	D ○	E ○	F ○	G ○	H ○
19	A ○	B ○	C ○	D ○	E ○	F ○	G ○	H ○
20	A ○	B ○	C ○	D ○	E ○	F ○	G ○	H ○

Part 5

21	A ○	B ○	C ○	D ○
22	A ○	B ○	C ○	D ○
23	A ○	B ○	C ○	D ○
24	A ○	B ○	C ○	D ○
25	A ○	B ○	C ○	D ○
26	A ○	B ○	C ○	D ○

Continues over

OFFICE USE ONLY - DO NOT WRITE OR MAKE ANY MARK BELOW THIS LINE

Draft

For Part 6:
Write your answers clearly in the spaces next to the numbers (27 to 32) like this:

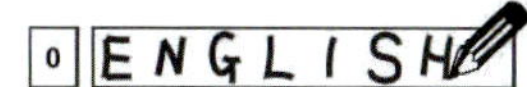

Write your answers in CAPITAL LETTERS.

Part 6		Do not write below here
27		27 1 O 0 O
28		28 1 O 0 O
29		29 1 O 0 O
30		30 1 O 0 O
31		31 1 O 0 O
32		32 1 O 0 O

OFFICE USE ONLY - DO NOT WRITE OR MAKE ANY MARK ABOVE THIS LINE

Cambridge Assessment English

Candidate Name		Candidate Number	
Centre Name		Centre Number	
Examination Title		Examination Details	
Candidate Signature		Assessment Date	

Supervisor: If the candidate is ABSENT or has WITHDRAWN shade here O

Preliminary Listening Candidate Answer Sheet

Instructions

Use a PENCIL (B or HB). Rub out any answer you want to change with an eraser.

For Parts 1, 2 and 4:

Mark one letter for each answer. For example: If you think **A** is the right answer to the question, mark your answer sheet like this:

For Part 3:

Write your answers clearly in the spaces next to the numbers (14 to 19) like this:

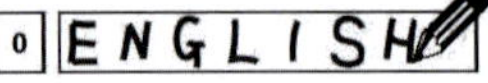

Write your answers in CAPITAL LETTERS.

Part 1			
1	A O	B O	C O
2	A O	B O	C O
3	A O	B O	C O
4	A O	B O	C O
5	A O	B O	C O
6	A O	B O	C O
7	A O	B O	C O

Part 2			
8	A O	B O	C O
9	A O	B O	C O
10	A O	B O	C O
11	A O	B O	C O
12	A O	B O	C O
13	A O	B O	C O

Part 3		Do not write below here
14		14 1 O 0 O
15		15 1 O 0 O
16		16 1 O 0 O
17		17 1 O 0 O
18		18 1 O 0 O
19		19 1 O 0 O

Part 4			
20	A O	B O	C O
21	A O	B O	C O
22	A O	B O	C O
23	A O	B O	C O
24	A O	B O	C O
25	A O	B O	C O

OFFICE USE ONLY - DO NOT WRITE OR MAKE ANY MARK BELOW THIS LINE

B1 PRELIMINARY

Writing

Sample Test

Candidate Name	

Centre Number						**Candidate Number**					

Answer Sheet for Writing

INSTRUCTIONS TO CANDIDATES

Write your name, centre number and candidate number in the spaces above.

Write your answers to Part 1 and Part 2 on this answer sheet.

You **must** write within the grey lines.

Use a pencil.

Do **not** write on the barcodes.

PV1

Practice Test 1 • Speaking

Part 2

Candidate A

Speaking Part 2

Practice Test 2 • Speaking

Part 2

Candidate A

Practice Test 1 • Speaking

Part 2

Candidate B

Speaking Part 2

Practice Test 2 • Speaking

Part 2

Candidate B

Practice Test 3 • Speaking

Part 2

Candidate A

Practice Test 4 • Speaking

Part 2

Candidate A

Practice Test 3 • Speaking

Part 2

Candidate B

Practice Test 4 • Speaking

Part 2

Candidate B

Practice Test 5 • Speaking

Part 2

Candidate A

Speaking Part 2

Practice Test 6 • Speaking

Part 2

Candidate A

Practice Test 5 • Speaking

Part 2

Candidate B

Practice Test 6 • Speaking

Part 2

Candidate B

Speaking Part 2

UNIVERSITY PRESS

Great Clarendon Street, Oxford, OX2 6DP, United Kingdom

Oxford University Press is a department of the University of Oxford. It furthers the University's objective of excellence in research, scholarship, and education by publishing worldwide. Oxford is a registered trade mark of Oxford University Press in the UK and in certain other countries

First published in 2019

2023 2022 2021 2020 2019

10 9 8 7 6 5 4 3 2 1

ISBN: 978 0 19 411877 4 Student's Book
ISBN: 978 0 19 411876 7 Student's Book Pack

Printed and bound by Gráfica Maiadouro S.A. in Portugal

This book is printed on paper from certified and well-managed sources

ACKNOWLEDGEMENTS

Back cover photograph: Oxford University Press building/David Fisher.

The publisher would like to thank the following for permission to reproduce photographs: 123rf p.210 (top/wrangel); Getty Images pp.14 (top/Tim Robberts, top middle/Westend61, middle/Rob Lewine, bottom middle/Lane Oatey/Blue Jean Images, bottom/JGI/Jamie Grill), 18 (John Rowley), 28 (Landscapes, Seascapes, Jewellery & Action Photographer), 64 (top middle/Kay Fochtmann /EyeEm, middle/Cecilie_Arcurs, bottom middle/PeopleImages), 70 (Hill Street Studios), 84 (top/Hero Images, top middle/Mint Images/Tim Robins, middle/FatCamera, bottom middle/kali9, bottom/Carl Smith), 86 (Tetra Images), 104 (top/Zave Smith, top middle/Westend61, middle/skynesher, bottom middle/Tetra Images, bottom/CZQS2000/STS), 106 (Chris Winsor), 110 (Vostok), 124 (top middle/Tim Robberts, bottom middle/pixelfit, bottom/Andresr), 126 (Tomasz Zajda/EyeEm), 130 (PictureNet), 144 (top/Westend61, top middle/vgajic, bottom middle/Westend61, bottom/Image Source), 146 (Artur Debat), 150 (EmirMemedovski), 210 (bottom/filadendron), 211 (top/AzmanL, bottom/Hero Images), 212 (top/Klaus Tiedge, bottom/svetikd), 213 (bottom/Prasit photo), 214 (top/praetorianphoto, bottom/Yuri_Arcurs), 215 (top/PeopleImages, bottom/PeopleImages); Shutterstock pp.54 (top/Vasyl Shulga, bottom/Kzenon), 64 (top/Daniel M Ernst, bottom/goodluz), 66 (Skumer), 90 (RUKSUTAKARN studio), 124 (top/goodluz, middle/Felix Mizioznikov), 144 (middle/stockfour), 213 (top/Stock-Asso).

All illustrations by: Christos Skaltsas (Hyphen).